THE SECRET OF THE SAUCERS

.

Edited by Ray Palmer

Published by
AMHERST PRESS
1955

This is an E-Z-READ book
designed to preserve your eyesight.

With deep affection and gratitude for their understanding and loyalty, I dedicate this book to my loving wife, Mabel and my devoted sons, Raymond and Richard.

Contents

FOREWORD   i

THE DISK FROM ANOTHER WORLD .   .   1

I TRAVEL IN A FLYING SAUCER   .   .. 16

MY MEETING WITH NEPTUNE 37

"WE CAN APPEAR AND FUNCTION
    AS EARTHMEN, ORFEO!"   .   . 52

THE PAST IS NEVER DEAD! 58

AIRPLANES DO DISAPPEAR! ..   .   . 64⁻

FLYING SAUCER CONVENTION
    IN HOLLYWOOD 75

MY AWAKENING ON ANOTHER PLANET 84

THE TRIP EAST 114

NEPTUNE AGAIN AND PHENOMENA
    IN NEW JERSEY 120

I HAVE A VISION 133

HOW TO KNOW A FLYING SAUCER 145

STRUCTURE AND MOTIVE FORCES
    OF FLYING DISKS 154

THE TRUE NATURE OF THE
    SAUCER MYSTERY 160

THE SECRET OF THE SAUCERS

FOREWORD

Many persons have asked me why the space visitors should have chosen me for contact rather than some other individual whom they considered eminently better qualified for such a contact than myself. Why, they infer, should the space visitors have picked so insignificant a nonentity as I for their revelations?

In all humility I tell you that I too have asked both the space visitors and myself that very question many times. And it is only within recent months that I have begun to understand fully just why I was chosen. But this is not the place in this book to disclose the reasons for their choice. After you have finished the book, however, you will have the answer. It is up to you then to decide whether or not you agree with the saucer beings in their choice of contact.

Thus I shall begin by telling you something of my early life and the space visitors first contact with me back in the year 1946, when I was totally unaware that I first came under their observation.

My childhood was the usual happy, carefree childhood of most American boys. I joined in the less strenuous games, attended school and was fairly good in my studies, although I was always frail and in poor health. Fortunately, my family was in fairly comfortable circumstances and they and my two indulgent uncles saw to it that I always had the best medical attention available.

My youthful trouble was diagnosed as "constitutional inadequacy" and its symptoms were great physical weakness, lassitude, lack of appetite and malnutrition. Hence I tired very easily and the slightest physical effort often left me weak and exhausted. I suffered from severe migraine headaches and as I grew older it seemed at times that every nerve and muscle in my body ached with excruciating pain.

When I was in the ninth grade the doctors advised that I discontinue school and continue my studies at home. This arrangement was highly satisfactory with me, for I had always been intensely interested in all branches of science. At home I was able to devote my entire time to the study of these subjects.

With plenty of rest and on a weight-building diet I gained strength and within a year the doctors believed I was well enough to return to school. But as my family had suffered some financial reverses in the meantime, it was decided that it would be best if I went to work for a while. I heartily approved. My first job was with my uncle's flooring and stucco company. He hired me as an estimator-salesman as I was not equal to any heavy work. I liked the work and enjoyed getting out and meeting people. All in all I got along pretty well even though I was considered just a kid. In my spare time I continued to study all of the books I could get hold of on scientific subjects.

In 1936 I met Mabel Borgianini, an attractive Italian girl who is a direct descendant of the famous Italian Borgias. From the first, both of us knew that we were meant for each other. Her happy, cheerful disposition helped me to keep from brooding over my health and physical inability to accomplish all of the things that I longed to do. It was the happiest day of my life when we were married. About a year later our first son, Raymond, was born and our cup of happiness was full.

A little later I suffered a complete physical breakdown and was forced to give up my job. My weight fell alarmingly from 150 to 103 pounds and I was so weak that I could scarcely sit up. After a number of medical examinations and complicated tests, the doctors decided I was suffering from a neurovascular disturbance. They prescribed complete rest and continuous medical attention.

Thus I entered a new world, a white world of doctors, nurses and hospital beds. For eighteen long months I was confined to bed. My body was wracked with excruciating pains and I was so utterly exhausted that I could not even read. Medical science was doing everything possible for me, but I knew that my doctors didn't believe that I would ever pull through. Frankly, I didn't much care whether I lived or died. Life was no longer desirable. To lie day after day on a white hospital cot with a body flayed with pain and too exhausted even to think is indeed a living hell. Death, I felt, could only mean release from pain. Especially was the confinement difficult for me to bear as I had always loved the out of doors, the sparkle of the sunshine, the whisper of the leaves in the woods, and the music of the woodland streams. Sometimes I prayed that I might die and escape the pain and awful weariness that ached in my muscles.

But weeks lengthened into months and gradually I began to improve. Finally I was able to sit up again and then to walk. It was like being reborn. I even began to take an interest in my science books once more. At last came the joyous day when I was able to leave the hospital and return home. All through those long months of confinement the faith and encouragement of my wife and family never failed. Mabel was with me through it all and if it hadn't been for her love and understanding I doubt if I ever would have made it.

My body was still wracked with pain, but I had learned to bear that. The good thing was that the terrible exhaustion and trembling weakness was gone so that I was able to be up and about. Although my family tried to dissuade me, I insisted upon going back to work on my old job almost immediately. I had been inactive so long that I wanted more than anything just to be busy again.

After I returned to work, I took up courses in night school. The old insatiable hunger for knowledge was gnawing at my very soul. I realized that science had discovered much, but there were still so many things to be learned; so many of nature's secrets yet to be revealed. I was obsessed with learning the true nature of the atom; discovering a cure for the virus diseases and especially for polio, that most ghastly of all crippling diseases. I felt that a satisfactory explanation for the creation and operation of the entire universe was yet to be worked out. What was the great mystery of the creation of matter, or the actual origin of the atom? These and other similar enigmas echoed in my brain night and day.

The field of electricity and electro-magnetic phenomena interested me in particular. Probably because from earliest childhood I had an acute fear or phobia about lightning. During an electrical storm I suffered not only actual bodily pain, but mental perturbation and distress. Thus I became well versed in atmospheric static electricity.

I conducted some simple experiments on my own. I noticed that all fowl and especially chickens are nervous and apprehensive during an impending thunderstorm. It was obvious from my own reactions that they too experienced definite physical symptoms because of atmospheric conditions. Also, I discovered that chickens are subject to a "range paralysis" which in every respect parallels infantile paralysis in human beings. From my studies and experiments in this field I believed that I had discovered certain facts that might be highly significant in the treatment of polio. In my enthusiasm, I wrote a long, detailed letter on the subject to President

Franklin Roosevelt, who was then in the White House.

Through the efforts of President Roosevelt my theories were heard by Dr. John L. Lavan, Jr., Director of Research, National Foundation for Infantile Paralysis. Dr. Lavan was interested and referred me to Dr. Joseph Stokes of the Children's Hospital in Philadelphia who was working along the vitamin therapy line of treatment for polio. But I never called on Dr. Stokes. From what I learned of his work I knew that his ideas were directly opposed to my own theory that a certain vitamin of the B complex group was largely responsible for the nutrition of the polio virus. (This view has since been substantiated by all research in virology.)

Returning to my studies and home experiments, I became interested in fungi and the atmospheric conditions affecting them. I studied the wild mushrooms and the particular atmospheric conditions which resulted in their sudden, erratic growth. From the mushrooms I turned to molds. It was my belief that molds are a negative form of life which leech on living matter by an illusive, subtle process of mutation.

At that time we were well into World War II. Penicillin had been discovered, but it was yet only a magic word and a deep mystery to the public. No books or reports were available on the subject. But by then I was familiar with the characteristics of fungi. In my experiments I discovered that one of the most common molds could be made to produce chemicals indefinitely if kept in proper nutrition and temperature. It was then I decided to see what structural changes would occur in the mold *aspergillus clavatus* in the upper atmosphere.

On August 4, 1946 I took cultures of the mold in three stages of growth: embryonic, half mature and mature. I placed the molds in baskets and attached the baskets to eighteen Navy-type balloons and prepared to send them aloft. But through an unfortunate accident the balloons broke away prematurely, carrying the baskets with the molds aloft with no means of retrieving them. My long months of strenuous effort and careful planning were hopelessly lost.

Heartsick, I sighed heavily as I watched the balloons and my precious molds ascending higher and higher into the clear blue sky. It was a perfect day, just the kind of weather I had longed for to make my test, but now everything was irreparably lost.

My family and a number of friends and neighbors were with me watching the experiment. Also on hand were a reporter and a photographer from the *Trentonian,* the Trenton daily newspaper. Everyone was silent staring into the heavens watching the balloons growing smaller and smaller as they gained altitude. Everyone there and especially Mabel and my father-in-law knew how keenly disappointed I was. Mabel put her arm comfortingly about my shoulders and murmured: "It's all right, Orfie. You can try again."

It was then that my father-in-law, Alfred Borgia-

nini, noticed a craft in the sky and called out:
"Look! There's an airplane, Orfeo. Maybe it will
follow your balloons."

Everyone there saw the object and it was the
consensus that it had been attracted to the spot by
the group of ascending balloons. But as it hovered
and circled overhead, we were all soon aware that it
was no ordinary airplane. In the first place it
maneuvered in an amazingly graceful and effort-
less manner. Then as we gained a clearer view of it,
we were startled to see that it did not have the
familiar outline of any known type of aircraft. It
was definitely circular in appearance and glistened
in the sunshine. We looked at each other in surprise and bewilderment and the photographer tried
to get some shots of the thing. Mabel exclaimed:
"Why, I never saw such an airplane before! It's
round and it doesn't have any wings!"

Everyone agreed and we continued to stare as it
gained altitude and appeared to follow after the
balloons until it too vanished from our sight. For
several days afterward we discussed the strange object, but as in the case of most mysteries, we forgot
all about it within a week or two. Today, however,
any one of those persons who were with me that day
will vouch for the authenticity of that strange craft.

Since then I have learned that the occasion of the
launching of the balloons was the first time I came
under direct observation of the extra-terrestrials.
Although I never then dreamed of the significance
of the event, that was their first contact with me.

From that moment on for the next five years and nine months I remained under constant observation by beings from another world, although I was wholly unaware of it.

The state police force was appealed to and requested to be on the lookout for the eighteen lost balloons and their strange cargo. Also, local radio stations and newspapers publicized the loss of the balloons and requested anyone finding or sighting them to report to authorities. But nothing was ever heard about them and to all intents the eighteen balloons and the mold cultures vanished.

Several days after the loss of the balloons I stopped in at the Palmer Physics Laboratory at Princeton University to visit Dr. Dan Davis, head of the Cosmic Ray Department. Dr. Davis had always been most friendly toward me and was never too busy to take time out to help me with some of the technical problems that were always troubling me.

I told Dr. Davis and one of his aides about the experimental molds and their loss in the accident with the balloons. Dr. Davis regretted that I had not told him about my experiments beforehand, for he said that the laboratory would have been glad to supply the hydrogen gas for the experiment and otherwise help to reduce expenses. Also, he said he would have arranged to have the balloons traced by the chain of radar stations in the eastern section.

Princeton and its environs were literally heaven-on-earth to me, for it was one of the important homes of my beloved science. In the vicinity were such great institutions as Rockefeller Institute for Medical Research, the R.C.A. Laboratories, the American Telephone and Telegraph Co.; the Institute for Advance Study; the Heyden Chemical Corporation, producers of penicillin. And nearby were Rutgers University, E. R. Squibb and Co., Merck and Son and many others. Yes, I loved every inch of New Jersey with its marvelous institutions of learning and scientific research. But my love for the state was offset by my uncontrollable apprehensions of and physical anguish during the rather violent thunderstorms there. Thus when Mabel began to talk of moving to the West Coast where I'd heard there were few, if any, thunderstorms, I was easily persuaded to go along with her plans.

In November of 1947 my family, consisting of Mabel and I and my two boys, Raymond and Richard, started by automobile for Los Angeles. On the trip we stopped at Rochester, Minnesota where I had an appointment at the famous Mayo Clinic with Dr. Walter C. Alvarez, the modern Hippocrates of diagnostic medicine. I sincerely appreciated my tremendous good fortune at being granted time by this authority in the field of medicine, for many far more deserving than I have been unable to see this busy man.

Despite his fame and his importance in the medical world, I found him extremely modest and kindly. After a thorough examination he concluded that my condition was caused by an inherent con-

stitutional inadequacy in an extreme degree. It was
his opinion that the condition had been induced by
a childhood attack of trichinosis from eating con-
taminated, under-cooked pork. He said I was fortunate to have survived the acute attack. He advised me to get as much rest as possible and never
to engage in work that was not of my choice and
liking in order to minimize the burden on my
weakened constitution and nervous system.

At last we arrived in the Golden State on the
West Coast. Southern California was a delightful
new experience for both my family and myself. I
decided it was paradise indeed when I discovered
that it actually was practically free from electrical
storms. And my boys and Mabel were thrilled with
stretches of golden sand at the seashores, the mountains and the continuous semi-spring that prevails
there at all seasons of the year.

We spent five months in California sight-seeing
and enjoying the sunshine and the wonders of its
scenery. At the end of that time we had to return
to Trenton, as I had some unfinished business to
attend to there. But I had purchased a lot in Los
Angeles and we planned to return and make our
permanent home there as soon as possible.

For some years I had been working on a thesis
titled, "The Nature of Infinite Entities" which included chapters on such subjects as Atomic Evolution, Suspension, and Involution; Origin of the
Cosmic Rays; Velocity of the Universe, etc. While
I was in Trenton I had the thesis published entirely

at my own expense and mailed copies to various universities and individual scientists working on fundamental research. Of course I realized at the time it was presumptuous of me, but I was completely carried away with my tremendous enthusiasm for ideas which I believed I understood but could not properly formulate because of lack of technical training.

It was my deep and abiding hope that some one of the scientists might understand what I was driving at and work out the technical and mathematical angles. Some of the men were interested, but none as far as I know ever exerted the effort on the theories that I had hoped they might. But at least I was satisfied that I had done my best considering the limited circumstances of my education. I was content to let the matter rest. It was obvious science had no need of me, a rank and presumptuous amateur. I must remain mute, an orphan of science!

We were all happy to return to Los Angeles and settle down in our new home. There I went into business with my father. But from the first we encountered vicissitudes on every side. For three long, difficult years we struggled along trying to make a go of it, but monopolies and stiff competition made the going so rough that we were finally forced to close down the business.

The temptation was great to return to the security of Trenton where material comfort and a small fortune awaited us if we would make our home there. But Mabel and the boys loved Southern

California. As far as I am concerned, security has never been of great importance in my world of the atom, the electron and the photon. Also, there were still those electric storms to reckon with. To an electrophobe like myself, this aspect is always of primary consideration. So we decided to forget security and gamble on keeping our home and making a go of it in Los Angeles where we were all content.

This was in the year 1948 and the flying saucers were then making headlines from time to time. But I was completely disinterested in the phenomenon. Like many other persons, I thought the saucers were some new type of aircraft being secretly developed here in the United States. I figured the information would come out in good time.

For several months I worked as manager of the Los Feliz Club House. In my spare time I endeavored to write a motion picture script. It was more of a hobby than anything else. I didn't really expect the script to be accepted as I'd had no writing experience. As the idea of space travel was quite popular in the films then, I concentrated on a story about an imaginary trip to the moon. Several studios were interested in the finished manuscript, but it was never made into a motion picture.

When the club house where I was employed was finally leased to a large organization, I made application for work at the Lockheed Aircraft Corporation plant at Burbank, California. The application was approved and I went to work for Lockheed on April

2, 1952, in the metal fabrication department.

After about six weeks in Metal Fabrication I was transferred to the Plastics Unit at Lockheed. Since plastics had always interested me, I was pleased with the change. I was one of a three-man crew working on radomes, or plastic and glass housings for the radar units of the F-94C and F-94B Starfire jet aircraft. I liked my fellow workers, Davé Donnegan and Richard Butterfield. Both were honest, sincere, hardworking typical young Americans. They had their feet firmly on the ground and although interested in new ideas and scientific developments, they were strictly on the material plane and not interested in abstractions.

I was fortunate indeed to have two such men to cushion the shock of the fantastic chain of events in which I was so soon and unexpectedly to be involved. As I look back now it appears that an occult power of some sort had neatly arranged every smallest detail in advance including the particular type of job I was in as well as the two men who were to be closest to me through all of my incredible experiences. Ours was the swing shift. The unusual hours appealed to me as well as the excitement of the new work and the motley assortment of people at the plant. But I did not know then what infinitely strange destiny fate held in store for me.

CHAPTER I

THE DISK FROM ANOTHER WORLD

Friday, May 23, 1952, was an ordinary day in Burbank, California insofar as I was concerned. I got up at my usual time, worked around the yard for a few hours and later stopped in at the Drive-In snack bar. After several cups of coffee and an exchange of good-natured banter with some of the customers, I left and went to my job at the Lockheed Aircraft Corporation plant.

Things went along well enough during the earlier part of the evening, but about 11 o'clock I began to feel ill. An odd prickling sensation was running through my hands and arms and up into the back of my neck. I had a slight heart palpitation and my nerves were on edge. I felt just as I always do before a bad electrical storm. As the familiar symptoms increased I went outside expecting to find heavy threatening clouds, but the night was exceptionally clear and the stars were bright.

Puzzled, I went to work wondering what was wrong with me. By 12:30 A.M., when the quitting whistle sounded, I was so exhausted I could scarcely stand; it would be a relief to get home and into bed. I took my car from the Lockheed parking lot and headed southeast on Victory Boulevard toward home.

I became increasingly conscious of nervous tension

as I drove. I sensed a force of some kind about me. Never in all of my similar illnesses had I experienced such peculiar symptoms. There was no pain, yet I felt as though I might die at any moment. The prickling sensation had increased and spread to my arms, legs and up into my scalp.

Frightened, I wondered if an old illness was returning upon me. Was I going to be confined to my bed again with the terrible debility and excruciating pain of the "constitutional inadequacy" of my schoolboy days? The dread symptoms were certainly there.

At Alameda Boulevard I stopped for a traffic signal. It was then I noticed that my eyesight was glazed and the sounds of traffic were oddly muffled and far-away as though my hearing was also affected. I decided that I had better stop at one of the all-night cafes and have a cup of coffee. But at the thought all of my alarming symptoms increased. I forgot the idea of a cup of coffee. My sole and overwhelming desire was to get home as fast as I could.

I continued on Victory Boulevard toward home. I had the illusion that the night was growing brighter as though enveloped in a soft golden haze. Directly ahead and slightly above my line of vision I saw a faintly red-glowing oval-shaped object. At first it was so dim I had to stare at it to be certain it was really there. But gradually it increased in brilliance. It was about five times as large as the red portion of a traffic light. Nervously I rubbed

my eyes; something was wrong with my vision! **But**
the thing remained there; not sharp and clearly
defined, but fuzzily luminous, definitely oval-shaped
and deep red in color.

I continued on Riverside Drive directly toward
the object, but it appeared to be receding from
me so that I remained relatively the same distance ⹁
from it. As it was almost one o'clock in the morning
there was little traffic on the road. Apparently no
one else had noticed the object as I saw no cars
stopped to investigate. I wondered if I also would
have missed it above the glare of the headlights if
my strange symptoms had not drawn my eyes to it.

I drove across the bridge over the Los Angeles
River with the object still in view. Just the other
side of the bridge, to the right of the highway, is a
lonely, deserted stretch of road called Forest Lawn
Drive. The object stopped and hovered over the
intersection. As I drew near, it gained in brilliance
and its red color grew deeper and more glowing.
Simultaneously, the physical symptoms I was ex-
periencing became more acute. I was aware of a
tingling sensation of pain and numbness in my
arms and legs that reminded me of contact with an
electrical current.

Now the disk veered sharply to the right off the
highway and began moving slowly along Forest
Lawn Drive. For the first time it occurred to me
that the fantastic thing could be one of those flying
saucers I had read about. I turned my car onto
Forest Lawn Drive and followed the object.

About a mile further along the disk swerved to the right, away from the road, and hung motionless over an unfenced field some distance below the road level. I drove off the pavement about thirty feet to the edge of the declivity. From there the glowing red disk was directly in front of me and only a short distance away. As I watched it in bewilderment it pulsated violently; then shot off into the sky at a 30- or 40-degree angle and at very great speed. High in the sky to the west it decelerated abruptly, hung for a moment; then accelerated and disappeared like a meteor.

But just before the glowing red orb vanished, two smaller objects came from it. These objects were definitely circular in shape and of a soft, fluorescent green color. They streaked down directly in front of my car and hovered only a few feet away. I judged each to be about three feet in diameter. Hanging silently in the air like irridescent bubbles their green light fluctuated rhythmically in intensity.

Then, apparently coming from between those two eerie balls of green fire, I heard a masculine voice in strong, well-modulated tones and speaking perfect English.

Because of the nervous tension I was under at that moment, amounting almost to a state of shock, it is impossible for me to give a verbatim account of the conversation which followed. The invisible speaker obviously was endeavoring to choose words and phrases which I could understand, but there

were several things which even now are not clear
to me. I can only make a poor approximation of
the gist of his words.

I do, however, remember the first words spoken
which were: "Don't be afraid, Orfeo, we are
friends!" Then the voice requested that I get out
of my car and "Come out here." Mechanically, I
pushed open the car door and got out. I didn't
feel fear, but I was so weak and shaky that I could
scarcely stand. I leaned against the front fender
of my car and looked at the twin pulsating circular
objects hovering a short distance in front of me.

The glowing disks created a soft illumination,
but I could see no person anywhere. I remember
vaguely that the voice spoke again calling me by
my full name in words of greeting. It further stated
that the small green disks were instruments of
transmission and reception comparable to nothing
developed on earth. Then the voice added that
through the disks I was in direct communication
with friends from another world.

There was a pause and I dimly remember thinking that I should say something, but I was stunned
into utter silence. I could only stare in fascination
at those fantastic balls of green fire and wonder if
I had lost my mind.

When the voice spoke again I heard these startling
words: "Do you remember your eighteen balloons
and the mold cultures that you lost in the skies back
in New Jersey, Orfeo?"

I was astounded to hear the strange voice recalling

an incident out of the past which had happened so long ago that I had almost forgotten it. "Yes . . . . yes sir, I do!"

"Do you also remember the strange, wingless craft that appeared to be observing your activities?"

Suddenly the entire scene came back to me crystal clear in memory. I remember Mabel, my wife, my father-in-law and our friends and neighbors with me as we stared at that strange, disk-shaped object in the sky. I recalled how the object had appeared to follow the balloons bearing my precious cultures of *Aspergillus Clavatus* mold. I had been quite an experimenter in those days. It was then it dawned upon me that the fluorescent disks were similar in shape and behaved in the same erratic manner as had that mysterious craft back in New Jersey. The only difference was that I had seen the craft in daylight when it glistened like metal whereas the disks glowed in the darkness.

"You do remember us, Orfeo," the golden voice stated. "We were observing your efforts that day as we have watched you since then."

All traces of fear left me at these words, but I could not help but wonder what it all meant. Suddenly I realized that I was feeling very thirsty.

As though in response to my thought, the voice said: "Drink from the crystal cup you will find on the fender of your car, Orfeo."

Astonished at his words, I glanced down and saw a kind of goblet on the car fender. It glistened in the soft light. Hesitantly I lifted it to my lips and tasted the drink. It was the most delicious beverage I had ever tasted. I drained the cup. Even as I was drinking a feeling of strength and well-being swept over me and all of my unpleasant symptoms vanished.

"Oh thank you, sir," I said as I placed the empty cup back on the fender of my car only to see it disappear.

At that moment another incredible phenomenon began to occur. The twin disks were spaced about three feet apart. Now the area between them began to glow with a soft green light which gradually formed into a luminous three-dimensional screen as the disks themselves faded perceptibly.

Within the luminous screen there appeared images of the heads and shoulders of two persons, as though in a cinema close-up. One was the image of a man and the other of a woman. I say man and woman only because their outlines and features were generally similar to men and women. But those two figures struck me as being the ultimate of perfection. There was an impressive nobility about them; their eyes were larger and much more expressive and they emanated a seeming radiance that filled me with wonder. Even more confusing was the troubling thought somewhere in the back of my mind that they were oddly familiar. Strangely enough, the projected images of the two beings appeared to be observing me. For they looked directly at me and smiled; then their eyes looked about as though taking in the entire scene.

I had the uncomfortable feeling as they studied me that they knew every thought in my mind; everything I'd ever done and a vast amount about me that I didn't even know myself. Intuitively, I sensed that I stood in a kind of spiritual nakedness before them. Also, I seemed to be in telepathic communication with them, for thoughts, understandings and new comprehensions that would have required hours of conversation to transmit, flashed through my consciousness.

Before those two incredible Beings I felt that I was only a shadow of the shining reality I sensed them to be. It is difficult to express my feelings in words, for my understanaing of them was gained primarily through intuitive perception.

After several moments the two figures faded and the luminous screen vanished. Again the two disks flamed into brilliant green fire.

Trembling violently from weakness and cold perspiration, I was on the point of blacking out when I heard the voice again. It was more kindly than ever as it said something about my being understandably confused; but it assured me I would understand everything that had happened later on. Also, I remember these words: "The road will open, Orfeo."

I didn't understand. Instead the thought flashed through my mind: "Why have they contacted me; a humble aircraft worker — a nobody?"

The voice replied: "We see the individuals of Earth as each one really is, Orfeo, and not as perceived by the limited senses of man. The people of your planet have been under observation for centuries, but have only recently been re-surveyed. Every point of progress in your society is registered with us. We know you as you do not know yourselves. Every man, woman and child is recorded in vital statistics by means of our recording crystal disks. Each of you is infinitely more important to us than to your fellow Earthlings because you are not aware of the true mystery of your being.

"From among you we singled out three individuals who, from the standpoint of our higher vibrational perception, are best fitted for establishing contact. All three are simple, humble and presently unknown persons. Of the other two, one is living in Rome and the other in India. But for our first contact with the people of Earth, Orfeo, we have chosen you.

"We feel a deep sense of brotherhood toward Earth's inhabitants because of an ancient kinship of our planet with Earth. In you we can look far back in time and recreate certain aspects of our former world. With deep compassion and understanding we have watched your world going through its 'growing pains'. We ask that you look upon us simply as older brothers."

The voice continued, speaking rather rapidly. It stated that they were well aware that the flying saucers had been treated humorously by most people — as it was meant they should be. In this way they wanted the people of Earth to become only gradually aware of them and grow accustomed to the idea of space visitors. It was best that we receive them lightly at first for the sake of our own stability!

The voice stated that the disks were powered and controlled by tapping into universal magnetic forces; thus their activated molecules received and converted energy inherent in all the universe. It further explained that the complexities of the apparently simple structure of their disks were so great that to an Earthling a saucer would be considered as having "synthetic brains", although each one is to a degree under the remote control of a Mother Ship. Also, most of the saucers, as well as the space craft of other planetary evolutions, are of a circular shape and vary in size from a few inches to hundreds of feet in diameter.

A disk, the voice continued, is able not only to relay whatever is transmitted to it from a Mother Ship, but also it records precisely all visual, auditory and telepathic impressions that come within the scope of the disk. These impressions are relayed to the Mother Ship where they are permanently recorded upon what Earthlings would popularly term "synthetic crystal brains". Thus for centuries had been recorded a detailed account of Earth's civilization and the spiritual evolution of individual persons.

The voice also stated that in addition to the remotely controlled saucers there also existed space ships, some of which had been seen by Earthlings. It was further explained that the Etheric entities in reality had no need of space-craft of any type and when they were employed by them it was only for purposes of material manifestation to men.

I distinctly remember the voice making some such statement as this: "Interplanetary ships and saucers of various material densities can approximate the speed of light. This seems impossible to you only because of a natural principle which has not yet been discovered by your scientists. Also, the Speed of Light is the Speed of Truth. This statement is presently unintelligible to Earth's peoples, but is a basic cosmic axiom.

"Approaching the speed of light, the Time dimension, as known upon Earth, becomes non-existent; hence in this comparatively new dimension there are incredibly rapid means of space travel which are beyond man's comprehension. Also, within the Records of Light are to be found a complete history of Earth and of every entity which has incarnated upon it.

Many of the saucers — of highly attenuated densities of matter — were invisible to Earthly eyes and could only be detected by radar. Also, any of the saucers could be rendered invisible at any time, or could be disintegrated by either explosion or implosion. Thus Earthlings had seen some apparently burst in a blue or white flash while others seemed simply to vanish in the air.

I remember wondering about Captain Mantell and several others who believed they had contacted the saucers. In reply to my thought I heard these words: "Captain Mantell was not pursuing the planet Venus. He was endeavoring to overtake and capture one of the remotely controlled disks. His death was absolutely unavoidable!

"We wish to tell Earth's people that visitors from other planets occasionally visit Earth's dense, heavy, gaseous atmosphere. All are of kindly intent and none will harm man. All intelligences capable of space travel can read thoughts and see emotions. Man believes himself civilized, but often his thoughts are barbaric and his emotions lethal. We do not say this as criticism, but state it only as fact. Thus it is best to approach all planetary visitors with friendly, welcoming thoughts!"

As I listened to his words I wondered why these incredible beings hadn't landed several space ships at one of our large airports and thus convinced the world simply and quickly of their reality.

In answer, I heard these words: "That would be the way of the entities of your Earth, Orfeo, but it is not our way. Primarily because we function in dimensions unknown to man and hence interpret all things differently. Also, because there are planetary and cosmic laws as implacable as the natural laws of Earth.

"Cosmic law actively prevents one planet from interfering with the evolution of any other planet. In other words, Orfeo, Earth must work out its own destiny! We will do everything in our power to aid the people of Earth, but we are definitely and greatly limited by cosmic law. It is because the life evolution in its present stage of material advancement upon Earth is endangered that we have made our re-appearance in the atmosphere of your planet. The danger is far greater than Earth's people realize. The 'enemy' prepares in vast numbers and in secret."

For a moment the voice was still and then it said gently: "Among the countless other worlds in the cosmos, Orfeo, the children of Earth are as babes, although many of them believe they are close to the ultimate of knowledge. Among the worlds of the universe are many types of spiritual and physical evolutions. Each form of intelligent life adapts itself to the physical conditions prevalent upon its home planet. Most of these evolutions exist in more highly attenuated forms of matter than upon Earth. But the majority are rather similar to man in appearance. There is a definite reason for this being so. In reality, we are Earth's older brothers and thus we will aid Earth's people insofar as they, through free will, will permit us to do so."

As I listened to that kind, gentle voice I began to feel a warm, glowing wave of love enfold me; so powerful that it seemed as a tangible soft, golden light. For a wonderful moment I felt infinitely greater, finer and stronger than I knew myself to be. It was as though momentarily I had transcended mortality and was somehow related to these superior beings.

"We'll contact you again, Orfeo," the voice said. "But for now, friend, it is goodnight."

The two shimmering green disks faded almost out; then I heard a low hum as they flamed brilliantly into glowing green fire and shot up into the sky in the direction taken earlier by the larger red disk. In an incredibly short time they too had vanished, leaving me standing alone by my car.

Bewilderment, incredulity, shock and stark fear flooded over me — sudden conviction that I had lost my mind and gone raving mad. What I had witnessed, I felt, just couldn't have happened.

I raised my numbed hand and it was trembling violently. I saw by my watch that it was almost two o'clock in the morning. I climbed shakily into my car and kicked the starter. Panic was mounting in me. I twisted the steering wheel, gunned the engine and made a sharp, fast U turn to get back onto the road. The tires screamed and the car lurched.

I wanted to get home quickly. I wanted to get back to the world of sane reality. I wanted someone to assure me I wasn't going mad.

I drove with only a single objective in my mind — to get home! When finally I made the turn onto Glendale Boulevard and saw the lights of my apartment I breathed a heavy sigh of relief; no place had ever looked so good to me!

I left the car in the driveway and ran into the house. My wife was waiting up, worried and anxious because I was so late.

"Orfeo, what's the matter? What's wrong? You're white as a sheet!"

I stood staring at her, unable to speak.

She came to me and grasped my hand. "Orfeo, you're sick! I'm going to call a doctor."

I put my arms around her. I wanted only to feel her close to me and for the moment to try not to think of what I had been through.

She pleaded with me to tell her what had happened.

"Tomorrow — maybe tomorrow, Mae, I can tell you . . . ."

Finally we got to bed, but it was almost dawn before I drifted into a troubled half sleep.

CHAPTER II

I TRAVEL IN A FLYING SAUCER

I spent nearly all day Saturday in bed. The shock of my fantastic experience was so great that I found it difficult to get back to actualities. I kept having the feeling that the world I knew was a phantom world inhabited only by shadows.

It was not until Sunday that I could bring myself to tell my wife what had happened to me. I was afraid she would think I had lost my mind. Thus it was with relief I heard her say: "If you say it happened like that, Orfeo, I believe you. You've always told me the truth. But this thing is so strange and frightening — and you looked so deathly white when you came in."

I could only put my arms around her as I replied: "It scares me too, Mabel — I don't know what to think!"

Sunday afternoon I took my twelve year old son Richard and drove back to the spot on Forest Lawn Drive where I had seen the disks. There in the loose dirt I found the deep skid marks the tires of my car had made Friday night.

Richard looked at me curiously and asked what I was looking for. I pointed to the skid marks and told him that was the spot where I had seen what could only have been a flying saucer. Richard stared incredulously. "But dad, I thought you always laughed at people who believed in those things."

"You're right, son," I replied. "But that was only because I didn't know any better. Friday night I saw three of the saucers from this very spot."

Richard's eyes widened with interest. Then he began shooting questions at me so fast that I had to ask him to slow down. But I was glad he did not doubt my word.

Seeing those skid marks where I had gunned my car in panic to get away from the eerie spot assured me of the reality of my experience. I was convinced that I had been in contact with beings from another world.

Monday night I went back to my swing-shift job at Lockheed. It felt good to be back at work again! The friendly banter, laughter and jokes of my co-workers were just what I needed.

Beyond my family I told no one of that first experience, as I knew I would be ridiculed. In fact even at home very little was said about the saucers or my experience, for the subject invariably upset my wife and filled her with such apprehension that even the boys refrained from talking much about it.

But when I was alone I thought long and often about those incredible beings from that other world. The voice had promised: "We'll contact you again, Orfeo." I wondered when they would get in touch with me again and how? Had they meant soon — or would it be months or even years? These and hundreds of similar questions clamored in my mind.

I wondered if I was under constant observation

by them. If so, I thought that through telepathy I could signal them to return. One night I went back to that lonely spot on Forest Lawn Drive and tried to establish telepathic communication. But it was useless! No glowing red disk appeared — only the night and the empty skies that gave back no answer.

Weeks passed and still no further sign from them. Doubts began to trouble me. Time dulled the memory of that night and I began to wonder if my experience had actually been real after all.

Then early in July there began a fresh flood of well-authenticated sightings of saucers in the skies over Southern California. Local newspapers carried banner headlines announcing FLYING SAUCERS OVER LOS ANGELES! Some people were convinced we had interplanetary visitors and looked for mass landings at any moment.

Later in the month additional sensational sightings were reported from many other States. It seemed the skies were filled with the baffling mystery objects that defied all natural laws and behaved more like phantoms than material realities. As I avidly read each new account I became convinced anew that I knew the secret of the flying saucers. But I longed for more knowledge. I hoped and prayed for another contact with those incredible beings I had seen so briefly that Friday night.

July 23, 1952 I didn't go to work. I wasn't feeling well and believed I was coming down with the flu. I was in bed all day, but in the evening I felt a little better and thought a walk in the fresh air would be good for me.

I walked down to the snack-bar at the Los Feliz Drive-In theatre, several blocks from the eleven-unit apartment-court where we live. The small cafe has a warm, friendly atmosphere and it gave my spirits a big lift to listen to the small talk and friendly ribbing. Because of the many recent newspaper reports, the talk turned to flying saucers.

Ann, one of the waitresses, laughingly remarked that she couldn't get enough sleep as her husband insisted upon staying up most of the night watching the sky with binoculars trying to get a glimpse of a saucer. This brought on a round of flying saucer jokes and everyone was laughing, including myself. The fact that I could laugh indicates that I had pretty well gotten over the shock of my experience.

When I'd finished my coffee I left the snack-bar and started home. It was a little after ten o'clock. Beyond the theatre is a lonely stretch of vacant lots. The place is eerie and forbidding at night, for huge concrete buttresses rise from it supporting the Hyperion Avenue Freeway Bridge several hundred feet overhead. The bridge casts dense, oblique shadows down below making it a shadowed no-man's land.

As I crossed the vacant lots in the deep shadows of the bridge a peculiar feeling came over me. Instantly I remembered that sensation — the tingling in my arms and legs! I looked nervously overhead but saw nothing. The feeling became more intense and with it came the dulling of consciousness I had noted on that other occasion.

Between me and the bridge I noticed a misty obstruction. I couldn't make out what it was. It looked like an Eskimo igloo — or the phantom of an igloo. It seemed like a luminous shadow without substance. I stared hard at the object. It was absolutely incredible — like a huge, misty soap bubble squatting on the ground emitting a fuzzy, pale glow.

The object appeared to be about thirty feet high and about equally wide at the base, so it wasn't a sphere. As I watched, it seemed to gain substance and to darken perceptibly on the outside. Then I noticed it had an aperture, or entrance like the door to an igloo, and the inside was brilliantly lighted.

I walked toward the thing. I had absolutely no sense of fear; rather a pleasant feeling of well-being. At the entrance I could see a large circular room inside. Hesitating only an instant I stepped into the object.

I found myself in a circular, domed room about eighteen feet in diameter. The interior was made of an ethereal mother-of-pearl stuff, irridescent with exquisite colors that gave off light. There was no sign of life; no sound. There was a reclining chair directly across from the entrance. It was made of that same translucent, shimmering substance — a stuff so evanescent that it didn't appear to be material reality as we know it.

No voice spoke, but I received the strong impression that I was to sit in the chair. In fact, a force seemed to be impelling me directly toward it. As I sat down I marveled at the texture of the material. Seated therein, I felt suspended in air, for the substance of that chair molded itself to fit every surface or movement of my body.

As I leaned back and relaxed, that feeling of peace and well-being intensified. Then a movement drew my attention toward the entrance. I saw the walls appeared to be noiselessly moving to close the aperture to the outside. In a few seconds the door had vanished, with no indication that there had ever been an entrance.

The closing of that door cut me off entirely from the outside world. For an uncomfortable moment I felt utterly alone — lost to my family and friends. But almost immediately a pleasant warmth passed over me giving me once more that feeling of peace and security. I breathed deeply and found the air cool and fresh. Vaguely I wondered what was going to happen next.

Then I thought I heard a humming sound. At first it was almost inaudible, but it grew to a steady, low-pitched rhythm that was more like a vibration than a hum.

Next I was aware that my body seemed to be sinking more deeply into the soft substance of the chair. I felt as though a gentle force was pushing against the entire surface of my body. It was a peculiarly pleasant sensation that put me into a kind of semi-dream state.

While the humming sound increased I noticed that the room was darkening as though a heavy shadow was engulfing the room in twilight. As the light diminshed I began to grow apprehensive. I had the realization of how alone and helpless I actually was. For a bad moment I was on the edge of panic in the tightly sealed, darkening room.

Then . . . I heard music! It seemed to be coming from the walls. I couldn't believe my ears when I recognized the melody as my favorite song, "Fools Rush In". The panic within me subsided for I realized how safe I was with them — they who knew my every thought, dream and cherished hope!

Reassured, I settled back to enjoy the music. In a few seconds the interior of the room began to grow light again. Soon it was more brilliantly lighted than ever. It was at that moment that I noticed a glittering piece of metal on the floor of the craft. It was the shape and about the size of a quarter. I reached down and picked it up. It was different from any kind of metal I had ever seen, for it seemed almost to be alive in my hand. It quivered and began to glow almost like a live coal; yet it remained at the same temperature as my body. Now I noticed that the piece of metal was diminishing in size. It was as though some mysterious kind of sublimation or degeneration was taking place before my eyes. Could it be that contact with my hand was causing the substance to dissipate into the air? I placed it back upon the floor of the craft. There it ceased to quiver and the odd glow was no longer apparent.

I leaned back in the chair and noticed my soiled, faded work clothes which I had worn when I went to the snack-bar. The coarse fabric appeared crude and glaringly out of place in the exquisite, shimmering mother-of-pearl room.

"Where are they taking me?" I wondered, as I half listened to the music. For I was certain that the craft I was in must be moving. Were they taking me to their world, or was I going to spend eternity lost in space in that pearly igloo?

While I was still pondering these questions I felt the push against the surface of my body lessen, then cease altogether. The music stopped playing and the humming vibration in the floor died away too. I was certain that whatever type of motive power was used was housed somewhere below the floor as the faint vibratory hum definitely came from there.

Then smoothly and noiselessly the chair made a quarter turn toward the wall. Even as much as I trusted my unseen friends I was a little frightened at this. Tensely I waited, gripping the arms of the chair. Directly in front of me a circular opening appeared in the wall about six feet in diameter, but everything appeared hazy through it.

As I stared, the lights inside darkened. Then either the entire craft or the seat turned slightly more to the left and the strange window widened about three more feet. I saw a huge globe surrounded with a shimmering rainbow. I trembled as I realized I was actually looking upon a planet from somewhere out in space. The planet itself was of a deep, twilight-blue intensity and the irridescent rainbow surrounding it made it appear like a dream vision. I couldn't see it all, for a portion at the bottom of the sphere was cut off by the floor line.

Now I heard that voice I remembered so well. "Orfeo, you are looking upon Earth — your home! From here, over a thousand miles away in space, it appears as the most beautiful planet in the heavens and a haven of peace and tranquillity. But you and your Earthly brothers know the true conditions there."

As I listened to the tender, gentle intonations of that wonderful voice an overwhelming sense of sadness came over me. I felt tears in my eyes — I who had not know the relief of tears since I was a small boy. My heart was so full of emotion that tears were the only possible expression. They flowed unheeded down my cheeks. I was not ashamed for the tears seemed somehow to cleanse and purify me and to break down the hard, unfeeling, crystalized shell of The Reasoner that I had come to pride myself upon being.

The voice said softly: "Weep, Orfeo. Let tears unblind your eyes. For at this moment we weep with you for Earth and her Children. For all of its apparent beauty Earth is a purgatorial world among the planets evolving intelligent life. Hate, selfishness and cruelty rise from many parts of it like a dark mist."

The words brought fresh tears to my eyes as I thought of conditions on Earth and how they must appear to these perfected, compassionate beings who had extra-dimensional sight.

There was silence for a moment. Then I noticed that the room was apparently revolving away from Earth. Gradually the heavens came into view — an awesome, breathtaking sight from that tiny craft. All space appeared intensely black and the stars incredibly brilliant, set like jewels against black velvet — large, small; single and clustered. I felt lost in a strangely beautiful, ethereal world of celestial wonder.

All was brooding silence, order and indescribable beauty. A deep feeling of reverence possessed me. I had never been an actively religious man, but in that moment I knew God as a tangible, immutable Force that reaches to the furthest depths of Time and Eternity. And I felt assurance that the beings in whose care I was at that moment were close to the Infinite Power.

For a moment there was deep silence. Then as I wiped away the tears I saw a fantastic object coming slowly into view through the "window". It resembled a dirigible except that it was definitely flattened at the bottom. It emerged gradually into view from the right.

I studied it closely, wondering at its composition. It did not appear to be metallic like an airplane, but was definitely crystalline and gave the illusion of transparency. Its light properties definitely suggested perfect crystal alloyed throughout. I surmised it might be some sort of crystal-metal-plastic combination. When the entire ship was in view it appeared to be at least 1000 feet long and about 90 feet thick, but it could have been a great deal larger for there was no way to judge how close I was to it.

I stared fascinated at the half-ethereal "ship", scarcely conscious that I was again hearing music. But as my ears caught a startling, unfamiliar, strain, I listened intently to music such as I had never heard or could imagine. It is beyond description, for it was not music as we know it, nor was it played to our musical scale. It was strange, haunting drifts of melody that brought visions of star galaxies and planets spinning in notes of perfect harmony.

The voice spoke again: "Brother of Earth, each entity of your planet is divinely created and immortal. Upon your world the mortal shadows of those entities are working out their salvation from the plane of darkness. Every person upon Earth and its adjoining planes of manifestation are definitely arrayed upon either the positive side of progression toward good, or on the negative side of regression toward greater evil. We know where you stand, Orfeo; but are you going to be content to drift as you have been?"

"No . . . . oh, no!" I replied impulsively. "I want to work constructively. Only grant me strong physical health and there isn't anything I shan't be able to accomplish."

The voice replied gently. "That wish we cannot grant you, Orfeo, as much as we might like to. It is only because your physical body is weakened and your spiritual perceptions thereby keener that we have been able to contact you. Had you been physically in robust health with your mortal body and mind perfectly attuned to the sluggish lowered vibrations of Earth, we could not have manifested to you.

"Sickness, ill-health and all mortal afflictions are transient and unreal. They, along with pain, sorrow, suffering and conflict make up mankind's lessons in the school of the world where wisdom and spiritual evolution are gained primarily through suffering. An explanation of this terrible enigma will be given to you later. But tonight we tell you that you can rise above the inadequacies of your physical body, Orfeo, as may all other Earthlings. Remember always that we love you and your brothers of Earth. We will do everything within our power for the children of Earth that they will permit us to do, through free will.

With these words, the huge ship I was observing began moving upward and toward the left. One large "porthole" after another opened in rapid succession as the ship ascended until what appeared to be three decks were visible and I could catch fleeting glimpses of the interior of the gigantic sky ship. The inside appeared to be of the same luminous mother-of-pearl substance as the interior of the craft I was in. But I saw nothing more, no sign of life, no furnishings or equipment such as we on Earth know.

As I watched the ship I realized that the voice as well as the ethereal music had actually originated in the great sky ship. It came to me then that this must be a mother ship and that beings in it had remote control over the movements of the saucers that skimmed and skipped through our atmosphere. It awed me to realize what a high degree of intelligence and what expert hands were behind the saucer phenomena. I felt ashamed of having pleaded for a healthy body, who had already been granted so much.

As the craft moved further out into space I noticed what appeared to be a rotor at each end of the ship. I say rotor, but actually the things appeared to be vortices of flame.

With my limited knowledge I judged these incredible disks of fire to be tremendously powerful power plants whose terrific energy could be diverted to almost any purpose. The disks I had first seen were used as radio transmitters and receivers; then as a huge three-dimensional television screen on which, through some method of telepathic contact, it was possible both to see and to hear. Now I saw those same disks apparently propelling the vast sky ship. It was my guess that just such a power plant had shot the very craft I was in a thousand miles out into space in a mere matter of minutes and without any discomfort to me. It was clearly evident that all of the bewildering and insurmountable problems of space travel that baffled our engineers and scientists had been overcome by these people to such an extent that the entire trip into outer space was as simple as a ride in an elevator.

I wondered if they had discovered the secret of resisting gravity with its counter-force; if not, then by what other means had they conquered or neutralized gravity? I remembered that Earth's scientists believed that a man in a space ship would be absolutely weightless and apt to float about. I lifted my hand and let it drop to the arm of the chair. It behaved precisely as it would have on Earth. There must be an artificial gravity induced in the floor of the craft.

I wondered too how they had overcome the menace of lethal cosmic rays, meteors, sky debris, etc. Surely my ship carried no tons of lead shielding scientists declared necessary for adequate protection from cosmic rays. Also, I wondered in what way they had mastered the terrific pressure and temperature changes so that I was never conscious at any time of variations in either? And their motive power; what was the fantastic secret of those green fireballs? Possibly they were vortices of magnetic power which operated almost silently and with astounding efficiency. What a wonder world their planet must be, I thought, as I gazed in awe at the crystalline dream-ship passing from my line of vision.

Slowly then the room turned back toward the left and the Earth appeared once more with its shimmering rainbow halo. Dimly I could make out the faint outlines of the Western Hemisphere in varying shades of misty blue. Also I could see faint puffs of light scatered here and there which I judged to be the larger cities of the North American continent.

Two flying saucers darted into view and sped downward toward Earth. Just as abruptly they decelerated and hung suspended in space as pinpoints of light. As I was wondering about them I heard the voice say that one was over Washington, D. C. and the other over Los Angeles. Los Angeles — the word echoed in my consciousness as I gazed at the faint brush of light that was a great sprawling city. I tried to remember that Los Angeles was my home, but it seemed only vaguely familiar; a place remembered somewhere in Time.

"Tonight, Orfeo," the voice continued, "you have explored a minute distance into the limitless highways of the universe. Through your own efforts the road may later be widened for you. Tonight you, an entity of Earth, have come close to the Infinite Entities. For the present you are our emissary, Orfeo, and you must act! Even though people of Earth laugh derisively and mock you as a lunatic, tell them about us!"

"I will . . . . I will . . ." I whispered haltingly knowing that everything I said was heard by them even as all my thoughts were known to them.

"We know you will, Orfeo," the voice replied. "Thus tonight a special privilege has been yours. We love the Children of Earth and it is our desire to help them as the hour of crisis approaches. But only through such harmless ones as you can we work.

"The aggressive men of Earth want our scientific advancements. For these they would shoot our crafts from the skies — if they could. But additional scientific knowledge we cannot give to Earth except as we are now doing in a manner perfectly in accord and harmony with cosmic law. Already man's material knowledge has far outstripped the growth of brotherly love and spiritual understanding in his heart. Therein lies the present danger. To add to the destructive phase of man's scientific knowledge is not permitted. We are working now to turn that knowledge to constructive purposes upon Earth. Also we hope to give men a deeper knowledge and understanding of their own true nature and a greater awareness of the evolutionary crisis facing them. At present we are working along all constructive lines of human endeavor and especially in the fields of medicine and healing. Surely you cannot fail to see the tremendous advances which have been made in this direction within the last few years. Even greater 'discoveries' are at hand including success in the fight against cancer. Thus shall we continue to work with and through men."

I listened to the compassionate voice, trying to imprint every word on my consciousness. But I have forgotten much and these words are only a poor attempt to recall all that I heard. The voice continued speaking:

"We know your mind is filled with questions. One question in particular troubles you and it con-

cerns the entity the world knows as Jesus Christ.
May we set your mind at rest. In allegorical language Christ is indeed the Son of God. The star that
burned over Bethlehem is a cosmic fact. It announced the birth on your planet of an entity not
of Earth's evolution. He is Lord of the Flame — an
infinite entity of the sun. Out of compassion for
mankind's suffering He became flesh and blood and
entered the hell of ignorance, woe and evil. As the
Sun Spirit who sacrificed Himself for the children
of woe he has become a part of the oversoul of mankind and the world spirit. In this He differs from
all other world teachers.

"Each person upon Earth has a spiritual, or unknown, self which transcends the material world and
consciousness and dwells eternally out of the Time
dimension in spiritual perfection within the unity
of the oversoul.

"In the illusion of Time is written man's choice
through free will whereby he set in motion the cause
of error which inevitably resulted in effect, in which
mankind entered mortal consciousness or the living
death of his present existence. Thus was he separ-
ated from his eternal and perfect self. His one purpose upon Earth now is to attain reunion with his
immortal consciousness. When this is accomplished
he is resurrected from the kingdom of death and
becomes his real immortal self made in the image
and likeness of God. Your Teacher has told you,
God is love, and in these simple words may be found

the secrets of all the mysteries of Earth and the worlds beyond."

Tears coursed down my cheeks. Under the spiritual scrutiny of that great, compassionate consciousness I felt like a crawling worm — unclean, filled with error and sin. Yes, I say sin, but not in the ordinary sense men use that word. Rather sin as sin really is. And basically sin is hypocricy, falsity, the living lie! It is looking at your fellow man with a friendly smile upon your face with treacherous, malicious, or mocking thoughts in your heart. Sin is any and all deviations from absolute truth, perfect love, absolute honesty and righteous motives. Thus actual sin has little to do with Earthly standards of sin.

As these realizations filled my consciousness I wanted to fling myself down upon the floor and hide my head in shame for humanity. And of all men I at that moment felt the lowliest, the least worthy to be where I was. I wondered how those great beings could love such a one as I or any of mankind. We with our bloody wars, our intense hatreds, our cheap, shoddy intolerances, our greed and avarice and our cruel inhumanity to our fellowmen. I hid my head in my hands and wept bitter tears for a creature so full of error and hypocrisy and yet so puffed up with egotistical pride over our little material knowledge.

At that moment, as in a dream, I heard the strains of the "Lord's Prayer", played as though by thousands of violins. As I crouched in the chair fresh tears poured from my eyes. My heart was filled with humility, contrition and with gratitude — gratitude that these Great Ones had even considered our miserable selfish existence.

Above the exquisite strains of melody, the voice said: "Beloved friend of Earth, we baptize you now in the true light of the worlds eternal."

A blinding white beam flashed from the dome of the craft. Momentarily I seemed partially to lose consciousness. Everything expanded into a great shimmering white light. I seemed to be projected beyond Time, and Space and was conscious only of light, Light, LIGHT! Orfeo, Earth, the past were as nothing, a dark dream of a moment. And that dream unfolded before my eyes in swift panorama. Every event of my life upon Earth was crystal clear to me — *and then memory of all of my previous lives upon Earth returned.* IN THAT SUBLIME MOMENT I KNEW THE MYSTERY OF LIFE! Also, I realized with a terrible certainty that we are all — each one of us — TRAPPED IN ETERNITY and ALLOTTED ONLY ONE BRIEF AWARENESS AT A TIME!

I am dying, I thought. I have been through this death before in other earthly lives. This is death! Only now I am in ETERNITY, WITHOUT BEGINNING AND WITHOUT END. Then slowly everything resolved into radiant light, peace and indescribable beauty. Free of all falsity of mortality I drifted in a timeless sea of bliss.

At last, as from a vivid dream, I regained con-

sciousness. Dazedly, I looked about the interior of
the craft. Everything was the same, but it seemed
ten thousand years had passed in what must have
been only a few moments. I was half conscious of
a burning sensation on my left side just below the
heart, but I thought nothing of it then.

Ethereal drifts of music were in the air. Far away,
I could feel, more than hear, a pulsing vibration
beneath the floor of the craft. Also, I was again
aware of the gentle push of my body against the
cushioned chair. I realized I was being taken back
to Earth.

In an incredibly short time the wall opened and I
saw the familiar surroundings. Yes, I knew I was
home again. But I also realized a little sadly that
Earth could never again really be my home. In
the spiritual evolution of mankind, I had been ex-
pendable in this life. Thus had I passed through
death and attained infinite life.

As I got up from the comfortable chair, I reached
down and picked up the strange, shining bit of
metal and carried it in my hand as I left the craft.
In a kind of daze I walked away from the ship; then
curiously turned to look at it from the outside once
more. But it was gone! I looked up and there it
was high in the sky, faintly visible as a fuzzy luminous bubble. Then suddenly it was not there at all;
but high in the northeastern sky I saw a red, glowing disk which changed to green and vanished.

I glanced down at the round bit of strange metal
in my hand. It was glowing and livid again and

appeared almost to be alive as it quivered in contact with my flesh. Also, it was rapidly diminishing in size. By the time I had reached home it had dissipated into nothingness.

As I was undressing to go to bed, I remembered again the burning sensation I had felt on my left side while I was undergoing the profound "initiation" in the saucer. I glanced down and saw what appeared to be a circular "burn" about the size of a quarter on my left side directly below my heart. The outer rim of the circle was red, inflamed and slightly raised as also was a small dot in the center of the circle — the symbol of the hydrogen atom. I realized they had impressed that mark upon my body to convince me beyond all doubt of the reality of my experiences in the cold light of the coming days.

CHAPTER III

MY MEETING WITH NEPTUNE

Following the emotional shock of that profound and bewildering trip in the saucer, I went about in a veritable daze for weeks. I continued on the job at Lockheed and resumed the routine of my daily affairs; but I was like an automaton — a dweller in two worlds and at home in neither. It is almost impossible to explain my state of mind. But the great spiritual illumination I had received in the saucer left me something of a stranger to my own planet, Earth.

I longed to tell the world, to blazen out the truths of my discoveries; yet I knew that for the greater part I must forever remain silent. Among other glimpses of reality, I attained the realization that TIME IS NON-EXISTENT. What we call Time exists only in the physical worlds and is an illusion of the senses. Also, I know now that our concept of space is entirely erroneous. But who could I convince of these and other truths — who would believe me?

But because THEY had requested that I tell Earthlings of my experiences, I told many persons about my trip in the flying saucer. Nearly everyone laughed and ridiculed me. I was the butt of numerous jokes. Someone was always wise-cracking: "Are your saucer pals going to show up tonight,

Orfeo?" Or: "Tell one of the saucers to land over at the Drive-In theatre, Angie, and then we'll all believe it!" Such remarks invariably brought forth gales of laughter at my expense. But I no longer cared — I KNEW, and that was enough!

As my story got around, several newspapers printed derisive accounts of "The Saucer Man". It cut deeply to see the embarrassment and humiliation it all caused my two sons. They knew people were saying their father was a "screwball". They didn't want to go to school because their companions laughed at them. I knew it all hurt Mabel too. Mabel pleaded with me to forget my experiences. I tried to explain to her why I had to tell about them, and we had some bitter misunderstandings on the subject.

I wanted so much to do something constructive, but I didn't know how to go about it. I began calling various military and defense offices. The personnel of several of the smaller ones laughed openly and passed me off, I know, as a crackpot. But it was with tremendous relief I found the really important offices referred me to men who were genuinely interested. They questioned and cross- questioned me concerning the information I gave them.

A little later I began giving weekly talks to small groups of interested people about space visitors. At first these meetings were held in private homes and then as the attendance increased we met in the Los Feliz Club House.

In what little spare time I had I began writing down my experiences and planned to publish them in a small newssheet, for I believed I could reach more people that way.

But as the days and weeks passed following my fantastic trip in the saucer and nothing more happened, I began to feel a little uncertain. The constant ridicule and laughter created even more doubts. My insistence upon the absolute truth of my experiences finally appeared to be definitely alienating my friends and even my family. My story was unbelieved upon Earth and the mysterious visitors were doing nothing to aid me. I actually began to doubt my own sanity, to wonder if the bizzare experiences had been an illusion or hallucination of some sort. And yet an inner tribunal of Truth assured me that such was not the case for WITH THEM I HAD SEEN AND KNOWN REALITY — and I could never forget that.

On the night of August 2nd I and Mabel were helping out at the Los Feliz Drive-In theatre snack bar. About 11 o'clock I went outside for a breath of fresh air. Over the hills to the west I noticed a fuzzy green light apparently hanging suspended in the sky. I watched it for several moments, then went inside and called Mabel and seven or eight others to come out and see it. All of them saw the mysterious light hanging motionless in the sky over the hill. Unable to explain it, some of them declared it must be a helicopter hovering in the air. Others thought it might be a high street lamp of some sort.

But when after three or four minutes the "street

lamp" climbed slowly and *silently* into the heavens
and suddenly vanished, no one had much to say.
But for some perverse reason none of them wanted
to admit that it was actually a flying saucer.

As they trouped back into the cafe laughing about
"Orfeo and his flying saucers", a depressing wave of
discouragement passed over me. It was useless —
absolutely useless — to talk to anyone about the
saucers or my experiences. Feeling greatly dis-
heartened and vey much alone, I decided to leave
and walk home.

As I cut across the vacant lots the Hyperion Avenue Freeway Bridge loomed huge and dark ahead
of me. The sky was overcast and the dense, oblique
shadows from the vast concrete structure were
heavier and more eerie than usual. Yet in the
shadows of the dark archways of the bridge I had
come to feel a kind of warmth and welcome, a spiritual communion with a vastly greater and more
kindly world. For it was in the shadows of the huge
bridge that I had come upon the saucer which had
carried me out of this world.

I was thinking of these things when I suddenly
became aware of someone approaching from out of
the darkness. I was startled for I'd never before
met anyone taking the short-cut beneath the bridge
so late at night. I was about to call out a word of
greeting when it dawned upon me that the stranger
was coming from the *dead end* of the bridge. My
first thought was that someone was lying in wait for
me, possibly to rob me. But before I could become

alarmed, I heard the stranger call: "Greetings, Orfeo!"

My heart almost stopped beating, for immediately I recognized the vibrant, beautiful voice of the being who had spoken to me in the saucer.

I stopped in my tracks, utterly speechless, and stared at the approaching figure. But then a wave of joy and gratitude flooded over me, and I finally replied falteringly: "Greetings . . . to you . . ."

, He laughed pleasantly. "I know that in your mind you have given me a name — I who have remained nameless to you," he said gently. "You may call me by that name, Orfeo — it is as good as any other and has more inner significance to you than any name I might give you."

"Neptune . . ." I spoke the name slowly and reverently. For it was indeed the name I had given to this great and mysterious being. Then I added: "At last you have come to give me strength and faith."

He was near enough then for me to see that he was several inches taller than I and similar in outline to a well-built man. But the shadows were so heavy that I couldn't make out the details of his figure. But just to be in his presence once more was to sense again a tremendous uplifting wave of strength, harmony, joy and serenity.

"Come, Orfeo," he said gently, continuing on past me. "We have many things to discuss tonight."

I followed him as he strode ahead of me through the dense shadows. I could hear his solid footsteps upon the gravelled path which convinced me beyond the shadow of a doubt that he was no phantom or illusion.

He led me to a better lighted area near the bend of Glendale Boulevard where it goes up and over the bridge. I was actually trembling in anticipation of my first actual look at the mysterious visitor from another world.

When he turned I saw his face, the same wonderful, expressive countenance I had seen on the luminous screen. I again noticed especially his extremely large, dark and expressive eyes and nobility and beauty of his features which actually seemed to radiate warmth and kindliness.

Then I noticed that he was wearing a kind of uniform, bluish in color, perfectly tailored and tightly fitted to the outlines of his body. But it was apparently without seams, buttons, pockets, trimmings or design of any sort. In fact it fitted so perfectly that it was almost like a part of his body.

But as I studied him I became aware of an astonishing phenomenon: I could see his uniform and figure clearly, but it wavered occasionally, as though I were viewing it through *rippling water*. And the color did not remain solid and uniform, but varied and changed in spots, which reminded me of an imperfectly tuned television set. Only his face and hands remained immobile and stable as though not partially obscured by a film of rippling water.

Headlights from approaching automobiles fell upon us from time to time and I remember wondering what manner of being my companion appeared to be to those in the passing cars. Did they see him at all? If so, did he appear as solid and substantial as myself?

He moved forward again, motioning for me to follow him. Without speaking he led me down the sharp concrete declivity into the bed of the dry Los Angeles River. There he sat down upon a large stone and motioned for me to do likewise.

For a time he was silent and I was acutely conscious of a tremendous vibrational field about him; a tangible emanation of serenity, brotherly love, and ineffable joy.

At last he said: "You sense and understand intuitively many things I cannot say directly to you, Orfeo. You have just fully realized that we are not like earthmen in that we function in dimensions unknown to your world. Earth is a three-dimensional world and because of this it is preponderantly false. I may tell you that to the entities of certain other worlds Earth is regarded as 'the accursed planet', the 'home of the the reprobate, fallen ones'. Others call your Earth 'the home of sorrows'. For Earth's evolution is evolution through pain, sorrow, sin, suffering and the illusion of physical death. Believe me, all evolutions are not similar to Earth's, despite the *present* beliefs of your scientists."

As I heard these strange words, my heart and mind cried out: "But why must it be so? Why should Earth's people know pain, suffering and death?"

He looked up into the heavens and in the soft light I saw deep compassion in his face as he said slowly: "The answer to that question is one of the mysteries of the illusion of Time. But I can tell you this: such conditions did not always prevail among the entities who now inhabit Earth. Once there was another planet in your solar system, the fairest and most radiant of all the planets. That planet was the original home of Earthlings. In their native home they knew no pain, sorrow, suffering, sickness or death. But in the glory and wonder of their world they grew proud and arrogant. They made war among themselves and finally turned against the Great Giver of Life. Ultimately they destroyed their own planet which today exists only as a sterile and barren ring of asteriods and debris in the solar system. In order that those entities might gain understanding, compassion and brotherly love they were born into the animalistic, material evolution of a lesser planet, Earth. Suffering, sorrow, frustration and death became their teacher. Their symbol became the Man-Beast. Each man must work out his own destiny and salvation. In the illusion of Time and through repeated births and deaths each entity slowly and painfully evolves spiritually toward its former glorified state of divinity. Eventually all the entities of Earth will again attain their lost heritage. They will have learned understanding, compassion and true love for God and their fellows."

I pondered his strange words thoughtfully, thinking as I did so that what he had said explained many

apparent mysteries about man and his lot upon
Earth. But soon my attention was distracted once
more as I saw the figure of Neptune strangely
"waver" again. Suddenly the question was in my
mind: "Was he really there in the truest physical
sense, or was he an immaterial projection into the
physical world from another dimension? Did I see
him in his true form and ordinary state of being, or
merely a projected approximation of a man's appearance?" These strange thoughts frightened me a
little and carried me into too deep waters.

A reassuring smile lighted his face. "Don't be
alarmed, Orfeo. The answer to the troublesome
question in your mind is both yes and no. On Earth
form, color, individuality and the material aspect
of things is all-important. In our world these il-
lusions are of practically no importance at all. Suf-
fice to say that for you I am an approximation of
myself as I really am. I can't make it any clearer in
three-dimensional terms."

I thought about my own troubled fellows of
Earth. Impetuously, I asked: "What about Earth
now? On the surface all seems fairly calm, but I
know we are only drifting on dangerous and treacherous waters. In their hearts many people are
troubled and afraid. There is the ever-constant fear
of the H-bomb and of other horribly destructive
weapons being developed in the laboratories. Also
there is the creeping menace of Communism that is
threatening the world, and so many other things. . ."

When Neptune spoke his voice was calm and

dispassionate: "Communism, Earth's present fundamental enemy, masks beneath its banner the spear-
head of the united forces of evil. Along with good,
all men have evil in their hearts to a degree. But
some are much more evil than others. Communism
is a necessary evil and now exists upon Earth as do
venomous creatures, famines, blights, tyrannies, cat-
aclysms — all are negative forces which awaken the
positive forces of good in man and cause them to
act. Thus are they combatted, understood and ultimately their unreality becomes apparent. For evil
is always eventually self-destroyed."

He paused and once more I noticed his "uniform"
darkening and lightening in spots, as though it were
made of restless pale bluish clouds and patches of
moonlight. Then I held my breath as he continued:
"Yes, war will come again to your Earth. We are
powerless to prevent it. Millions in your land will
fight to the end for their cherished ideals and freedom of the human mind, with only a minimum on
their side for victory. The hour of travail which in
future history shall be known as 'The Great Accident' is nearer than any man dreams. And already
the clouds of war are on the horizon, dark and
ominous; but overhead beams the rainbow, infinite
and eternal. Mankind will survive Armageddon
and awake to a new more glorious day of fellowship
and honest brotherly love. In the dawning great
New Age of Earth all will forget their bitter hurts
and build constructively together upon the solid
foundation of the Brotherhood of Man."

He stopped speaking and turned his radiant eyes full upon me. In the half-light his countenance was truly resplendent.

"There is not much more I can tell you now, Orfeo," he said. "Since the first publicized modern sighting of our disks in the year 1947, thousands upon Earth have come to believe in us. Many have actually seen our disks. Some have seen us clairvoyantly. Others have communicated with us clairaudiently. Still others recognize the truth of our existence and greater scope of our being, through intuitive perception. But as far as official proof of ourselves, for which so many clamor, we cannot offer that. Official proof of the existence of our disks will come. But for us to attempt physically to contact mankind through any so-called authoritative source would be only useless and possibly disastrous for them. Nearly all three-dimensional beings have no concept of, nor could they possibly understand, extra-dimensional beings. Tonight in visiting you I have broken a code — the code of 'hands off', as regards any interference in the affairs of Earth. Active cosmic law will see the necessary amends made."

He looked at me; his strange eyes suddenly saddened. For a moment I had the uncanny feeling that in his greater vision I appeared to him only as a fleeting, insubstantial shadow, utterly without reality as he knew it. In that revealing instant I knew that we of Earth are as far removed from their nature as Earth is from the Sun.

After a while he said: "I would shake your hand in token of our momentous meeting here tonight. But I cannot. I have gone too far already. For my transgression we must now recede an equal degree from you. The immutable law of cause and effect upon Earth will govern accordingly. As a result, but few will believe or even hear your account of our meeting. In the over-all picture your story will in no way change conditions upon Earth. Neither will any actual Earthly event be either hastened or retarded because of our meeting. At most your story will give only greater faith and inner conviction to the few — but it is an important few! The ways of God are immutable and apparent only to those who have spiritual discernment. In the illusion of Time all things will be fulfilled in their proper hour."

I found tnat I was trembling and my nerves fairly quivering. Whether from sheer emotion or actually from being within the vibratory range of Neptune, I don't know. I longed to thank him, to express the great feeling of gratitude in my heart; but I didn't know quite how. I said: "From the bottom of my heart I thank you, Neptune. I pledge my very life to you and the beings of your world, that greater understandings may come to mankind."

"We know you will not fail us, Orfeo," he replied. "No other contact may be made at this time. But have no further doubts about the reality of your experiences. The road is open now; walk it as you will. Your failure will be my own. But I smile upon

you for the increased numbers who will come to
know us in a truer aspect and to believe in us because of you. Strength and encouragement will be
given to the millions who will rise courageously to
meet the fiery trials ahead. I tell you this: the 'Great
Accident' is very close and the fury of the next war
will break when it is least expected; when men are
talking of peace. I cannot say more."

With these prophetic words, Neptune extended
his hand to me. But recalling his words, I did not
grasp it.

He smiled and his face actually seemed to radiate
light. "Orfeo, my brother!" he said with genuine
affection. "For my sake you refused to break the
code. My trust is forever in you, Orfeo. In your
simple action you have cleansed me from my contact with this ground."

He paused; then added: "Soon we shall recede
from Earth, Orfeo — and yet in reality we shall
never be far away. Later, we shall return, but not
to you, beloved friend. You will understand the
meanings of these words later on."

When I made no reply, he said: "I'm thirsty,
Orfeo. Perhaps you know where we might get a
drink of water?"

"Oh yes . . . . yes sir," I answered eagerly, getting
quickly to my feet. I remembered a small nearby
store that remained open all night. "Please wait
here; I'll be right back." I left him and clambered
up the embankment.

As I hurried toward the store, I turned and looked

back at the Hyperion Bridge. Beneath the high center arch I made out the hazy outline of a kind of ghostly "igloo" which I immediately recognized as a saucer similar to the one in which I had ridden.

At the store I bought two bottles of lemon soda and hastened back. But as I approached I was disappointed to see that the ghostly saucer was no longer beneath the arch of the bridge. Quickening my pace, I almost ran to the spot where I had left Neptune; but he was no longer there. I wasn't too surprised for I'd had a premonition he wouldn't be there when I returned.

I tossed the sodas away and sank down upon the ground. The place was appallingly desolate without him. I felt so acutely alone, so helpless and deserted —like a child left alone in a dark room when the light is suddenly extinguished. I looked upward and my eyes hopefully searched the skies. High in the western heavens I saw a soft, fuzzy green light which hung for a moment, then shot away and vanished.

"Farewell, Neptune," I said softly as I felt my eyes grow moist. "I know now Earth is not yet ready for a meeting with the beings from your world. But in the dawning of Earth's great New Age, that day will come, friend. When we have learned the meaning of true brotherly love; when we have overcome to a greater degree the evil inherent in our selfish hearts, then perhaps we will be worthy to meet the infinitely wiser and gentler brothers of your world. In those days your fellows will visit us openly and joyfully. No longer will Earth be 'the accursed planet — home of sorrows'."

CHAPTER IV

"WE CAN APPEAR AND FUNCTION AS

EARTHMEN, ORFEO!"

At first I told no one of my strange meeting with Neptune, for I knew only too well that my new story would meet with even greater disbelief and ridicule. But I immediately set to work writing down my further experiences. I had already placed my first experiences with the saucers in manuscript form and planned to publish it as the first edition of a small personal newspaper, *The Twentieth Century Times;* but I had experienced difficulty in finding a publisher. Now I was glad the paper was not yet in print, for I could include my most recent experience with Neptune.

I worked hard on the manuscript in my spare time. But the emotional and physical strain I was under began to tell on my health and I felt the return of many of my old symptoms of extreme weakness and fatigue. In October of 1952 I applied for a leave of absence from my job at Lockheed. This was granted and by an odd coincidence the first day of my leave started on the day the first strike in the history of Lockheed was called. I had the feeling that I had been saved from additional nervous stress and strain. Fortunately, the strike ended well and work resumed at the plant within a few weeks.

With time off from work, I was soon able to complete the manuscript. Also, with the additional rest, my health rapidly improved so that I was strong enough to return to work within a month.

The fellows at the plant knew of my interest in the saucers and many of them also knew of my first two experiences. I was in for a lot of ribbing from them. But on the whole it was goodnatured, friendly ribbing so I didn't mind. Several of those with whom I worked most closely frequently asked me for some kind of proof of the reality of my experiences. I told them of the shiny piece of strange metal I had picked up on the floor of the craft and explained how within a matter of minutes it disintegrated into nothingness. Also I told them of the burn I had received during my "initiation" in the saucer which had resulted in a mark on the left side of my chest. Some of them looked at the mark in the form of the symbol of the hydrogen atom. But these things were not sufficient proof for them.

One night at work several of them had been kidding me about my experiences. Al Sarradar quipped: "Just what kinda liquor you drinkin', Angie, that sends you outa this world?" Walter Seveicki chimed in: "Yeah, tell us so we can take a ride in a saucer too!"

We had just rolled out a heavy die. Al and I were removing the finished radome from it when suddenly there was a loud crackling sound as though a wooden plank had snapped. At the same instant I felt a shock in my right hand and a stinging sensation in my index finger.

The boys were startled. Al yelled: "What happened, Angie?"

I didn't reply, but held out my index finger for all of them to see. Five of them watched as a round welt appeared on my finger. The welt was not red like a burn, but appeared gray. It was about the size of a dime, a perfectly round circle with a dark dot in the center — again the symbol of the hydrogen atom.

Somebody said something about static electricity, but all of them were deeply puzzled, for nothing like that had ever happened before. Al advised me to get medical attention at the plant hospital. I told him it would not be necessary; there was no pain whatsoever. I reminded him that the same thing had happened to me in the saucer when I had received a considerably larger similar mark on my left side below the heart.

They laughed at my explanation and refused to believe that extra-terrestrials had anything to do with the sudden unaccountable phenomenon which had produced the strange mark on my finger. Yet they were mystified and today any one of them will testify to the authenticity of the experience. The odd mark remained on my index finger for some months as a constant reminder of the proximity of unseen visitors.

The latter part of October Mabel made a trip back to New Jersey to visit our folks. When she returned several weeks later my mother and father accompanied her, as they wanted to spend a month or two in California. Mabel wired me to meet them at the Greyhound bus depot.

I was eager to see Mabel again and looking forward to a reunion with my Dad and Mother. I drove downtown the night they were to arrive, as thrilled as a kid. It was around six o'clock and the streets heavy with traffic. Parking my car, I walked toward the bus terminal. It too was bustling with activity. In all of the excitement, flying saucers and space visitors were the farthest things from my mind. But as I entered the front door of the bus terminal I stopped in my tracks and stared, unable to believe my eyes. Directly in front of me and facing the newstand was a familiar face. I knew I couldn't be mistaken — it was Neptune!

He glanced up and his dark eyes told me that he was expecting me. He was dressed in an ordinary dark business suit and carried a brief case under his arm. A dark blue felt hat with snap brim shaded his eyes. And he appeared as real as any person in the depot! After the sudden shock of surprise I started forward to greet him, but a strong telepathic command stopped me. I stood hesitant looking at him. He stood up, facing me and I could not help noticing how tall, extremely handsome and distinguished he appeared in the hurrying throngs of people. He was not smiling; in fact, his face was almost stern as though he might be angry. I wondered what

I had done wrong. I completely forgot Mabel and the folks waiting for me.

His intent gaze never left me. Stalling for time I walked over to the newsstand and picked up a magazine and thumbed through it. I had received the definite telepathic impression not to approach him; thus I waited for him to speak to me. But he did not. Staring blankly at a page in the magazine I waited for further telepathic communication. It came! The gist of the message was: "The last time you saw me, Orfeo, I was in a less objectified projection in your three-dimensional world. The purpose being to give you some idea of our true aspect. But now tonight you see me fully objectified. If you did not know who I am, you could not tell me from one of your fellows. Tonight I am no half-phantom, but can move among men as an Earthman. It is not necessary for you to speak to me; you have gained the understanding. You know now that we can appear and function as human beings."

I looked gratefully into his eyes and as in my previous encounter with him, I felt again a unity of being as though I were momentarily released from the bonds of individuality.

Just then Mabel and the folks spied me. As in a dream I heard them call to me as they came rushing over to me. Like an automaton I kissed Mabel and hugged Mom and Pop. All the while they were talking and holding my hands. I was going through the motions of greeting them, but I was still so stunned that I scarcely knew what was happening.

Together we all walked toward the exit and I noticed that Neptune was following a short distance behind us. When we reached the door I was about to open it when Neptune reached out and pushed it open for us. I was more astounded than ever, for it meant that he could function in the physical world as easily as any Earthling.

Outside he walked a few paces to the left and stopped. There he opened his briefcase and removed a pack of cigarettes. He removed a cigarette from the pack and put the package back in the briefcase. Then without lighting the cigarette he tossed it into the gutter.

I was smoking a cigarette too. Following Neptune's action, I tossed my cigarette away. Mabel noticed my preoccupation and odd behavior. She looked at Neptune and then at me and asked: "Who is that man and why is he staring at us so intently?"

I didn't reply to her question as I was too confused to get involved in explanations. I said: "Come on Mae, let's get the suitcases into the car."

She knew something was wrong and I was aware of the three faces studying me with perplexity. I made fumbling excuses for my odd behavior. But on the drive home I was able to begin to snap out of it and to show them the warm welcome I felt in my heart.

CHAPTER V

THE PAST IS NEVER DEAD!

The Christmas holidays arrived with their gay, festive spirit and usual bustling excitement. By then things had settled back to normal and I had experienced no further contacts. Flying saucers seemed to have vanished from the skies; practically no accounts of sightings appeared in the newspapers. Although I had completed the manuscript for *The Twentieth Century Times*, I couldn't get up the courage to have it published.

Mabel kept saying: "Orfie, if you publish that, people will think you are completely crazy. Why don't you just forget it! Nothing good can ever come of it. Everything is going along so smoothly now; we're both working and the boys are happy — let's just leave it that way."

"But, Mae . . ." I'd remonstrate. "Don't you understand; these things really happened to me! It is my duty to tell what I know!"

"And just what thanks will you get for it? Do you want to be ridiculed, laughed at and considered a crackpot or a psycho? Think back! Remember how everybody talked when you first told that wild story about a trip in a flying saucer. What did it get you but ridicule! Even if it did happen, Orfie, forget it! Just forget the whole thing for your family's sake. Let's be happy and enjoy life."

Thus although I felt I was betraying Neptune, I let things drift and made no effort to get my story published. In fact on New Year's Day, 1953 our lives were going along so smoothly and pleasantly that I had decided to forget it all insofar as the world was concerned and let those incredible experiences become a part of the dead past of 1952.

But the events of 1952 would not rest. During the latter part of January, 1953 the front pages of the newspapers were carrying sensational new saucer stories. The Air Force released reports that flying disks and strange clusters of lights were numerous over Korea. F-94 Starfires had encountered several of the saucers and one of their pilots had gotten a radar magnetic lock on one of them. Northern Japan too had many sightings.

The reports made me restless. At night I frequently went outside and scanned the heavens. Frequently I saw the disks overhead as roving lights. Any casual observer would not give a second glance, but simply pass the lights off as ordinary airplane lights. And since our apartment was close to several large airports, there were usually airplanes visible at all times. I should never have been able to distinguish saucer lights from those of aircraft were it not for the peculiar sensitivity of my nervous system to the electro-magnetic effect of the saucers.

Then I began to be ashamed of myself for having failed so completely the trust that Neptune had placed in me. He had said: "The road will open, Orfeo; travel it as you will." I realized that thus far I had refused to travel the road and except for the few talks I had made to small groups I had done nothing to help people understand the strange visitors. More and more every day I realized how selfish I was in thinking first of my family and myself. Finally I knew there was no alternative for me. Come what may, I had to go ahead with publication of the facts of my experiences. It was the only constructive thing I could think of to do.

Without discussing the matter any further with Mabel, I took the manuscript for *The Twentieth Century Times* to several local publishers. None of them were encouraging. Far from it! The first one I approached was highly amused and a little contemptuous as he said: "You'd better send this thing to a science-fiction mag, old boy, unless you want to land in a strait-jacket."

The next publisher I tried told me how rambling and incoherently the thing was written. "You forget I'm not a writer, "I replied. "I've done the best I can and all of the facts are there."

He laughed. "You say the facts are here — but are they? You start off by saying these experiences are true and yet before the narrative is completed you have inferred several times that they could be imaginary. In fact, right here on the front page you make the statement: 'This story is either a yarn or it is real!' What kind of facts are those? And how can you expect people to accept the paper as actual fact?"

"I've thought of all that," I replied. "Frankly,

it was my idea to break the news gently. In other words, to let the readers feel uncertain at first as to the absolute authenticity of the facts. To tell this entire thing at first as fact is too much of a shock for an unstable world. As you yourself say, I might be hustled off to a mental institution. Let the truth of what I have to say develop gradually."

After considerably more talk along these same lines, he agreed to publish it, but only if I would permit him to edit it and delete major portions of the story. I flatly refused and he in turn refused to have anything to do with publication of the manuscript.

And so it went. I tried publisher after publisher with the same discouraging results. At last, however, I found a small publishing house that was willing to print the piece word for word as written if I would pay all publishing costs and take all of the papers myself. I agreed to do this. But as we parted he shook his head and said: "Pardon me for saying this, Mr. Angelucci, but I honestly think you are making a grave mistake. Not only are you throwing your money away, but you are liable to make yourself a public laughing stock."

"I'll have to risk all that," I answered. "There is no alternative for me; I must publish that paper."

Thus on February 19, 1953, the one and only issue of *The Twentieth Century Times* came off the press, an eight-page, tabloid-type newspaper which carried word for word an account of all my experiences I felt it was wise for me to release. I breathed a huge sigh of relief when I saw the paper, for I felt that I had satisfied a debt.

When I walked into our apartment with an armful of the papers Mabel took one horrified look at one of the sheets and sank down in a chair. "Oh Orfie, you didn't do it! You didn't! This thing is dynamite. It can wreck us. Wreck your job, my job and the boys' schooling. This can finish everything we've built up here."

"I'm sorry, Mae," I replied doggedly. "Believe me, there is no other way out for me. I've got to live with myself; so I had to do it. I hope you'll try to understand."

But I knew Mae didn't understand. And as copies of the paper got around, many of her predicted reactions occurred. People began ridiculing me outright and several papers published sarcastic news items about me and my experiences, subtly inferring that I "wasn't all there". Believe me, it wasn't easy to bear, and especially did I suffer for my family. The boys were ribbed unmercifully at school and at her job at the snack bar Mabel was the constant target for the sharp barbs of wit aimed at me.

But the response was not entirely negative. Some persons became genuinely interested. About that time I resumed my weekly talks at the Club House and thus I was able to distribute the papers at the meetings. As more and more persons became interested and ceased to take my *Twentieth Century Times* as a joke, I began to feel that all might not be lost. And more important, I could face my reflection in the mirror again, happy in the thought that I had not entirely failed the space visitors.

CHAPTER VI

AIRPLANES DO DISAPPEAR!

Not long after my publication of the paper a new aspect of my experiences with the saucers developed. On the afternoon of March 3, 1953 I was sitting alone in the kitchen, reading. I was dully aware of the steady drone of an airplane which continued for some time. The sound apparently was coming from the west. Gradually it dawned upon me that the sound was too steady and too unwavering for an ordinary aircraft.

Curiously, I got up and looked out the door. Coming from the north I saw what appeared to be an ordinary small aluminum airplane. From where I was standing in the doorway there was nothing unusual in the sound of the craft as it assumed the normal crescendo of direct approach. I stepped out of doors and watched it fly directly overhead until it was fairly in the face of the sun — when suddenly and astoundingly the plane was no longer there! Just as mysteriously the sound of its motor ceased abruptly too. I never saw the plane again. Confused, I went back into the house. Obviously the craft was not a flying disk, but a conventional type aircraft, for I had not experienced any of the unpleasant physical symptoms that a flying disk invariably produces in my body.

Four days later about five o'clock in the afternoon

I was accompanying Jane Vanderlick, a neighbor who is employed at the Loe Feliz Theatre cafe. We were walking to the cafe where Jane was going to open it half an hour early that day. We were laughing and talking when Jane noticed an airplane nearby in the sky, flying south. It seemed just an ordinary airplane of the most common type: "Maybe that's a flying saucer, Orfeo!"

I thought she was kidding me and replied: "Not you too, Jane!"

But her eyes were serious. "I mean it, Orfeo. There's something peculiar about that airplane."

For the first time I scrutinized the craft carefully. After a moment I had to admit there was something unusual about it. It appeared extremely dull and flat-surfaced and did not reflect any of the rays of the setting sun as it ordinarily should have done.

While we were both staring at it the airplane suddenly vanished right before our eyes in a clear and cloudless sky! The sound of its motor ceased just as abruptly. Both of us stood in our tracks. Jane stared at me. "What happened to that airplane, Orfeo?"

I shook my head and then replied slowly: "I wasn't going to mention it to anyone, Jane, but I saw the same thing happen four days ago. I don't know what it means!"

We stood there for some minutes our eyes vainly searching the skies for some trace of the vanished plane. I requested Jane to remember every detail of the strange incident. She promised that she would. If you ask her about it today, she will verify the experience just as I have related it to you.

Several days later I was with a group of employees sitting around the Lockheed Plant. It was about five minutes before four in the afternoon. We were waiting for the shifts to change preparatory to going on duty. My good friend, but most confirmed skeptic, Richard Butterfield, was with us. While we were talking idly, an apparently ordinary two-engine airplane came into view over the hills.

Butterfield's attention was attracted to the craft. He arose from the bench and stared up at it as though he was spellbound. His behavior reminded me immediately of Jane Vanderlick's actions a few days previously. Her eyes had been attracted to that particular plane just as Butterfield's eyes were now drawn to this one. Yet neither of the planes had any effect upon me. The crowd all noticed Butterfield's deep absorption in the small plane. Some of them started laughing and began ribbing him. I remember someone shouting: "Look! He ain't never seen an airplane before!" But Butterfield paid no attention. Finally, almost as though talking to himself, he said: "What is that?"

Several voices helpfully jibed in with wise-cracks about his being sorely in need of an optician's advice. One fellow remarked scathingly: "Any dope can see it's nothing but an ordinary two-engine airplane."

I didn't say anything, for I had noticed by then how flat-toned the craft was and how it failed to reflect the rays of the afternoon sun.

Suddenly there was an instantaneous flash that appeared to envelope the plane. When the flash was over there was no sign of a plane to be seen anywhere in the sky. The droning of its motors too had ceased. Many of the group had seen the phenomenon. They were startled and confused and everyone started talking at once trying to explain just what had happened. Others continued to stare into the skies searching for the vanished plane.

Butterfield dazedly brushed his hand across his eyes. It seemed difficult for him to come back to the norm of this world. He didn't say much, but for a long time after we had gone on the job he appeared to be in deep thought. I didn't volunteer any explanations, for the sudden disappearance of the plane in a brilliant flash was a new development for me. I kept mulling it over in my mind as well as the two previous experiences in which I had seen airplanes simply disappear into thin air. But I didn't give the incidents too much thought as I had more than enough to do to try and unscramble the puzzle of my previous experiences with the extra-terrestrials without adding more problems.

Within a week most of those who had seen the plane disappear had either forgotten the incident or had figured out some explanation that satisfied them. I saw then that the human mind does not want to believe anything it cannot understand; it will rationalize to any extent rather than face the unknown.

As the weeks passed I continued to be ribbed more

and more. Some of my fellow workers were even inferring that I was lying just for cheap publicity. I would joyfully have dropped the whole thing like a red-hot coal, if I had not had the deep sense of loyalty and responsibility to those Greater Beings that neither I nor my fellows could begin to understand.

As the situation became more unpleasant at the plant, I finally decided to turn in my notice; for by then my experiences were fairly well-known throughout Southern California and thus I was in for constant ridicule. I knew I'd either have to shut up about space visitors or else quit my job. I decided on the latter.

My last three weeks at work were rather memorable. On August 14th Ernie Oxford and I were working on an airplane part outside the building. He, like all of the others when they got me alone, was harping on the space visitors and my "wild story in that *Twentieth Century Times*." He was contentiously declaring that neither he or his girl friend could swallow such a story.

I told him that it was his right to believe only what he wished to believe. Then I suggested that we forget the subject and concentrate on the job we had to do. But Ernie couldn't be stopped. He kept on telling me what a big mistake I was making.

While he was berating me, I looked toward the Burbank mountains and there directly over a ridge top was a flying saucer. I touched Ernie on the shoulder and pointed to the saucer. He dropped his tools and stared. Don Quinn, working nearby, saw us gazing into the sky and came running over.

While we were watching the thing it appeared suddenly to "flip" and vanished. Ernie kept asking: "Where did it go?" And after that experience he was quiet for a while. Then he began talking about the saucers and nothing else. He still didn't believe my story, but he knew he had actually seen a saucer.

Friday, August 21st, at 9:15 in the evening, the entire shift was hard at work. My mind was preoccupied and I was busy on an airplane part. Suddenly a tremor passed over me. I knew it could mean only one thing. I put down my tools and walked to the huge door, which was open only about a foot. As I looked out into the night I saw a light in the skies which appeared to be approaching the plant. While I watched, the light stopped in midair and changed from amber to red. There was no doubt in my mind about what it was.

I called to some of the fellows in the plant and beckoned them to join me. A number of them hurried over and we pushed open the door and went outside. All who came were rewarded. Every one of the men saw the red disk hanging overhead in the sky. While they were staring I glanced at their faces and I was deeply impressed with what I saw. Momentarily, they were like changed men. Wonder, awe, and belief were in their faces. Thus I was struck with the realization of what the mere sight of a single disk can do to the thinking of a number of persons.

While I was watching their reactions, they all turned suddenly and looked questioningly at me. I glanced up into the sky to see that the disk had vanished and only the moon and the stars were overhead. I asked where the disk had gone and all of them started to tell me.

From the many explanations I learned that the saucer had appeared to move until it was directly below the moon where it began to ascend. As it ascended it changed in color from red to amber and then to the silvery color of the moon. As it climbed higher its color became indistinguishable from the moon so that they could not tell what actually happened to it. But it had vanished. All of that had happened while I was watching their faces.

We trouped back in to work and all of the men were quiet and thoughtful. At the ten minute break I told them that on the following night at the second break I was going to ask each one of them to tell his story of what he had seen.

Every man told precisely the same story. In all there were twelve men. I failed somehow to get the names of two of the fellows but here are the names of the other nine: Dave Donegan, Al Durand, Dave Remick, Michael Gallegos, Richard Becker, Richard McGinley, Bruce Bryan, Ernie Oxford and Louis Pasko. Every one of these men will affirm the details of this sighting. The phenomenon did not happen fast; they all had plenty of time to observe and impress details on their minds.

All of them believed they had seen a flying saucer.

Hence, I was enabled to leave my job with much of the stigma of untruth taken from the account of my experiences I had printed in all good faith in my *Twentieth Century Times*.

Among those twelve men there are two who are still deeply perplexed. They are Ernie Oxford and Michael Gallegos, for they had seen me drop my tools and go to the door as though beckoned by an unseen force. They said I behaved as though I were under a spell. Both of them started involuntarily to follow me, but on second throught remained on the job until I called them to come out.

Both of them insist that I must have received a message of some kind from the disk. When I told them that it was only a physical reaction and a deep intuitive feeling that space visitors were near, they believed I was holding something back from them. For they said that for a moment they too had felt something indescribable. With that I agree fully and I was happy that I was no longer alone.

Friday, August 28th was my last work night at Lockheed. I was outside working on an airplane part. That night Don Quinn was my partner. He was among those most skeptical of my saucer experiences and like the others he always insisted upon talking about them when we were together. He was telling me what a big mistake I was making in giving up my job and getting myself generally ridiculed. But I was used to such talk, and let him talk on. I glanced up into the sky and saw a silvery disk moving southeastward along the mountain rim.

I immediately called Don's attention to it. He dropped his tools and stared and immediately began demanding to know what it was. "Why does it behave that way?" "How can it hang in the air like that?" I didn't reply to any of his questions.

Suddenly, it too just disappeared. Poor Don stared at me incredulous and bewildered. He admitted its flight characteristics were like nothing he had ever seen or heard of; yet he would not fully go along with the flying saucer explanation. Actually, he could not quite believe his own eyes. Thus seeing is not always believing. For I have seen other persons actually see a saucer and refuse to believe the evidence of their own sight.

It was during August that many of the strange events included in this chapter occurred. It was also in August that a revealing press release came through International News Service which recalled to my mind those cases of the airplanes which mysteriously vanished in thin air. The news item follows:

PLANES SEEN OVER ARCTIC

Washington, Aug. 1 (INS). An Air Force spokesman disclosed today that roughly twelve unidentified airplanes have penetrated the U. S. defense perimeter in the Arctic within the last year.

The spokesman said that the "invaders" were not identified as Russian so no protests could be made to Soviet authorities.

Some of the planes were tracked on radarscopes while others were seen to give off white vapor streaks. But before U. S. fighter pilots could give chase, they would mysteriously disappear out of radar range, the spokesman said.

He asserted that the "raiders" crossed the edge of the U. S. radar perimeter in Greenland and Alaska, but added they also flew elsewhere over the North American continent.

The Air Force has given pilots strict orders not to fire upon any unidentified plane unless a "hostile" act has been committed or is about to be, such as a bomber flying over U. S. territory with its bomb-bay doors open.

Could it be that those mysterious "disappearing airplanes" I had seen had penetrated the U. S. defense perimeter in the Arctic?

On the following day a counter-release came through International News Service. This counter-release negated all of the information given out in the first release.

These contradictory reports followed an already definitely established pattern. Official news releases of a mystifying nature concerning the saucers are invariably followed up by counter releases or actual retractions of previous statements.

As irritating and confusing as such contradictory reports are to the public, nevertheless this method of handling UFO information by the authorities is best for everyone concerned. For with a little thought, it is clear that such mystifying news stories without an official damper placed upon them immediately, might easily flare up into a nationwide

conflagration of panic and hysteria. Official head-
quarters would be snowed under with avalanches of
telegrams, letters, phone calls and personal inquiries.
Thus only further confusion would result.

The story of the extra-terrestrials is one that no
one can or will ever be able to finish with any degree
of finality. It is my sincere personal belief that the
Air Force and other responsible offices have responded to and handled the problems of space visitors
precisely as those visitors have anticipated and de-
sired them to do. As more and more thinking persons realize this significant fact, we will be prepared for greater revelations to come.

Perhaps it would be well to state here that in the
cases of disappearing aircraft I do not believe the
ships dematerialize or dissolve into nothingness, as
it would appear. Being composed primarily of a
crystalline substance the ships may give the illusion
of complete transparency or, if so controlled, they
can be rendered entirely opaque. Thus, also, they
can manifest any color or combination of colors,
depending upon the energy employed and its control on the molecular substance of the crystal body.

It is no problem for the crystal disks to project
visual images of ordinary aircraft and similarly to
produce the auditory vibrations of aircraft engines.
These projections may be easily picked up on a radar
screen.

CHAPTER VII

FLYING SAUCER CONVENTION

IN HOLLYWOOD

During those last days I was at Lockheed I thought often of Neptune's cryptic words: "The road will open, Orfeo; walk it as you will." And later when he said: "I smile upon you, Orfeo, for your greatly enhanced numbers."

Then his last prophetic words, "Strength and courage will be given to the millions who will rise and meet the great battles ahead with only a faint hope on their side for victory."

It was true, I thought; the road was beginning to open. New understandings and an ever increasing awareness were coming to me as time passed. Also, as more and more people learned of my experiences many began to phone, write, or visit at our home, wishing to know more about the space visitors. We continued the regular weekly meetings at the Los Feliz Club House, but as the crowds increased, the Club House was no longer large enough to accommodate everyone. It was then that Max Miller, President of *Flying Saucers International*, an organization devoted to the study of flying saucer phenomena, and Jerome Criswell, the well-known columnist and television Man of Prophecy, suggested that we rent the music room in the famous old Hollywood Hotel for our weekly meetings. Thus we had been meeting there for several months every Sunday evening or afternoon. Opinions were exchanged and lectures on saucer phenomena were presented to enthusiastic audiences.

Paradoxically enough, as the general public's interest in the saucers increased, the press, radio, television and other news media suddenly and inexplicably dropped flying saucers from the news. Even the second-rate science fiction writers banished the word from their lexicon of horrors. Thus the public was left to grope for itself. And surprisingly enough the way was thus cleared for those individuals who had experienced actual contacts with the extraterrestrials to work freely without obstruction of erroneous "slanting" by official reporting.

Gerald Heard, Frank Scully and Donald Keyhoe were familiar names among persons interested in the saucers. These men, along with *Fate* magazine and Ray Palmer, had been making every effort to awaken the public to the awesome fact that our world might well be under observation by beings from another planet. But now several unknown men were speaking up and declaring that they had actually had contact with the saucers and space visitors. Among these were George Van Tassel, Truman Betherum, George Adamski, George Williamson and Alfred Bailey. Those few newspapers which ran stories on these men did so with the tongue-in-cheek slant.

Sunday afternoons I was speaking to groups at the

Hollywood Hotel. I knew that my audience waited patiently for clear, concise accounts of my experiences with extra-terrestrials. But they were often disappointed. Frequently when I stepped upon the platform to speak a strange transition came over me. It was as though another personality overshadowed me; someone who knew all of the answers. But the answers were not in my familiar English or Italian, but in an unfamiliar, half-remembered tongue. I would struggle to translate the ideas into English and end up by failing to be clear and direct. Thus with the understanding of the universe almost within my grasp, I was often helpless to reveal any part of it.

Nevertheless, even with my many failures to be concise and direct, the meetings gained momentum with increasing numbers in the audience.

It was then that Max Miller conceived the idea of a Flying Saucer Convention. It sounded like a tremendous idea to me. With the help of several other persons we enthusiastically began to formulate plans. It was decided that we should hold the convention at the Hollywood Hotel where there was plenty of room in the lobby to accommodate a large audience.

Various exhibits of saucer photographs, space ship models, books, magazines and pamphlets on the saucers were set up around the lobby and many circulars were mailed out announcing the event. Also invitations to speak at the convention were mailed to all persons who had been most helpful in revealing and disseminating information about the saucers and extra-terrestrials.

But response to the invitations was very poor. Less than a week before the convention was to open it appeared that none of the speakers whom we had counted upon would be present. Max was greatly worried. "It looks like we're sunk, Orfeo," he exclaimed dejectedly. "This thing is going to be the prize flop of any and all conventions."

But as I looked at him, the conviction was suddenly strong in my mind that everything would come off well. I replied: "Don't worry, Max. It's going to come off much better than we ever even dreamed it would."

My prediction proved entirely correct. Every one of the speakers whom we had invited showed up for the convention, and some others besides. Among the invited speakers were Frank Scully, Arthur Luis Joquel II, George Van Tassel, George Adamski, Truman Betherum, John Otto from Chicago, Harding Walsh and a mysterious Dr. "X" who spoke long and eloquently on the saucers. He left immediately after speaking and no one ever knew who he really was or where he came from, although many inquired; for he had some startling things to say.

Almost to a man the speakers said they had received an irresistible urge to attend on Friday (two days before the opening of the convention). Could it be that the space visitors had been at work in their own subtle way?

At any rate the convention was a tremendous success. For three days and night the crowds overflowed the Hollywood Hotel out onto the lawns and adjacent Hollywood Boulevard. In fact the response was so tremendous that on the second morning I requested Max to stop all publicity on the convention.

Some of the larger Los Angeles newspapers covered the convention. But all news stories were of the usual tongue-in-cheek type. A few of the smaller, more rabid papers tried to "expose" it as nothing but a promotional "money-making" scheme.

The convention was a hectic one. I was busy night and day and carried on practically without sleep. When I wasn't speaking, people were surrounding me and bombarding me with endless questions. Many were skeptical and did not hesitate to be belligerent about it. But all during my ten months of speaking at the weekly meetings and the three nerve-wracking days of the convention, I never once lost my temper. A power beyond my own consciousness or control carried me through. In trying moments of heckling or confusion an upsurgence of peace and calm would pick me up and give me strength equal to the occasion.

However, on the last night of the convention, the power that was sustaining me suddenly failed and I lost my temper for the first time. A lone woman who had been especially persistent in seeking me out and cornering me to revile me and hurl quotes of scripture at me was responsible for the outburst. She knew I was wrong and she was right. And she had books, diagrams and bible verses to prove it. When at last I literally blew my top she joyfully picked up her data and departed shouting that my temper proved I was an agent of the devil. Within an hour I lost my temper several times again.

The most trying experience of the convention occurred when a large group of materialists were literally "giving me the works" in a stubborn, derisive effort to "get at the bottom of my story" and ferret out obvious flaws from a "common-sense" viewpoint.

Sincere, open-minded, honest persons who are willing to investigate the advent of space visitors never resort to such sneering interrogations. They ask honest, sincere questions on points they do not fully understand. But they have an honest desire to know, not to discredit, to sneer and to disparage.

This particular group had their minds set upon "exposing" me. Their methods, although entirely on a mental plane, would make the medieval inquisitions seem innocuous. Like little demons they parroted elementary physics and could see practical, intelligent action only behind the Iron Curtain. They knew I was a cheap publicity seeker who did not hesitate to lie about space visitors or anything else to further my own ends. No words of explanation could possibly prove anything to them they did not wish to believe.

I had undergone just as bitter and insinuating

criticism before, but I was exceptionally tired that last night. I felt almost as though I were melting away before their venomous onslaught, collapsing at the seams, as it were, and suddenly I felt very, very human and down to earth. I was on the verge of exploding in anger again when a kind of veil was drawn over my conscious mind. The gesticulating figures before me faded to babbling, inconsequential shadows.

As they continued their violent attacks, my thoughts drifted calmly back to a scene of a few weeks before. I was attending a convention of science-fiction writers at the Hotel Commodore in Los Angeles. Since my experiences with the extra-terrestrials, I have become interested in the field of science-fiction, for I have found that many scientific truths are adumbrated, or delineated, in science-fiction before ever they become realities of our world.

Many well known writers in the science-fiction field were present. When I came in they were holding open discussions of trends in the science-fiction field, the various new markets, etc.

One of the audience asked: "Why have all science-fiction writers suddenly stopped writing or even mentioning flying saucers?"

A speaker replied authoritatively that the subject had become taboo with them.

Another member of the audience demanded to know why this was so since the saucers had actually given such an impetus to the science-fiction field.

The speaker had no adequate answer for that one, but lamely explained that the saucers were "old stuff" now.

I was becoming impatient with the proceedings and was on the point of leaving when the guest speaker of the evening was announced. He was Mr. Gerald Heard, the well-known science-fiction writer and author of IS ANOTHER WORLD WATCHING?

Mr. Heard spoke with great eloquence and a deep, penetrating philosophy. He berated the writers for turning out material of an inferior grade and warned that the public would not continue to "stomach it", much less to buy it. Many of them squirmed uncomfortably in their seats.

As he neared the end of his stimulating and thought-provoking talk, his eyes met mine where I was seated near the back with two companions. I noticed that he seemed tired and shaken.

As our eyes met and held, a kind of mutual understanding passed between us. It was as though vortices of light opened between us in ever widening circles. Dimly, I could hear him terminating his speech with these words: "There is one in this room tonight — I do not know who he is, but he's going to upset the whole applecart." He paused, then his voice reverberated as he added: "He is the Awakener — he has not yet appeared, but he well may be here in this very room tonight. Thank you."

And the mystic wheels between us set in motion

by the controlled magnetic vortices slowly receded and vanished.

I looked about the room at the audience, but they were no longer listening to him. Some were whispering and laughing among themselves.

As I looked about that busy room I thought that it was small wonder that the concoctors of science-fiction horror diets had declared the saucers "taboo". Far too much beautiful reality was on the side of the saucers. Harmony and beauty are much too tame for the horror boys. They have joined forces with the materialists, subversives and egoists to fight the "flying saucer sensationalists" down at every turn.

But the joke is on them, for reality has slipped quietly past them and established new frontiers of its own. The science-fictioneers were induced by subtle forces to ignore flying saucers as were many other materialistic sources of information. During the welcome lull the actual flying saucer phenomena and the extra-terrestrials were left to the inexperienced but honest handling of rank amateurs. At first these men were inept and inarticulate, but they are finding their voices and their numbers are rapidly increasing. The space visitors had actually only cleared the atmosphere for them. Had the professional spinners of horror-fiction stuck to the theme of flying saucers, the true contacts should never have been able to perform their missions.

CHAPTER VIII

MY AWAKENING ON ANOTHER PLANET

It was in the late summer of 1953 that the most beautiful and revealing of all of my experiences with the etheric beings developed. My life had been a kaleidoscope of new understandings and changing patterns since the night of my trip in the saucer, but apparently the most profound of all had to be revealed to my conscious mind in gradual steps of understanding, because the experience itself actually occurred in January of 1953 while I was still on the job at Lockheed, but it was not until six months later that I had any idea of the tremendous experience that had been mine. During those bewildering intervening six months I honestly believed that for seven days of my life in January, 1953 I had been a victim of complete amnesia. I told no one about it, not even Mabel, for so many confounding things had happened in the recent months of my life that I feared further complicating matters by relating an experience for which there seemed to be no explanation.

During those six months I experienced many very strange and disquieting hours. Vivid dreams of a hauntingly beautiful, half-familiar world troubled my sleep. Sometimes I would awaken trembling and bathed in perspiration feeling that I was close to conscious remembrance of an exquisitely beautiful experience that would explain many things. Also, frequently during the days, fleeting, tenuous memories drifted into the borderland of my consciousness.

Even more perplexing were those occasions when, while speaking to groups of persons at the Hollywood Hotel, I felt as though I were being somehow overshadowed by another greater personality; a personality who thought neither in my familiar English or Italian, but in a strange language which it seemed I once knew but now could no longer remember.

In order to clarify the experience itself, I must go back to that day in January, 1953 when it began. I did not go to work that afternoon as I was just recovering from the flu, but I was feeling so much better that I believed I could go back on the job the following day. Mabel was at work at the cafe and I was alone. About four o'clock a rather strange, detached feeling came over me. I was aware of a familiar odd prickling sensation in my arms and the back of my neck which usually announced the proximity of space craft.

I discounted the strange symptoms thinking they were only the result of my illness. Then suddenly I began to feel so drowsy that I could scarcely keep my eyes open. I remember starting toward the divan to lie down for a nap, but I later had absolutely no recollection of reaching that divan.

My next conscious perception was a peculiar "awakening" or regaining consciousness while on my job in the Plastics Department at Lockheed.

Stupefied and bewildered I looked uncertainly about the factory. Dazedly, I recognized the familiar faces of my co-workers . . . and noticed the tools in my hands. I caught my breath sharply and an icy shiver quivered over my entire body as quite involuntarily I recoiled with a shudder from the entire scene. I didn't know why then, but everything seemed hopelessly wrong, primitive and crude.

In a daze I rubbed a hand across my eyes hoping to eradicate the scene. Then I was seized with a blinding vertigo and thought I was going to lose consciousness. Dave Donnegan, my working partner, looked at me sympathetically, and there was genuine concern in his eyes. He didn't say anything, but quietly took the tools from my hand and in his quiet, understanding way went ahead, carrying on alone.

An involuntary outburst of utter disgust came from my lips, disgust with everything I saw. It seemed like the Dark Ages. I remember hearing Dave say: "Are you all right, boy?"

I didn't reply; I couldn't! In panic I turned to rush out of the door. In my bland haste I bumped roughly into Richard Butterfield, the temporary lead man in my section. I must have looked acutely ill because I vaguely remember seeing the alarm in his eyes as he grasped me firmly but gently by the shoulders and exclaimed: "Angie! Angie! What's wrong with you!"

I was breathing hard. Both emotionally and mentally I was confused and uncertain. My thoughts were in turmoil. I had only one objective; *to get out of that place!* But the presence of Butterfield had a stabilizing, quieting effect upon me.

He smiled reassuringly while keeping his hands upon my shoulders. "Calm down, Angie, old boy," he said gently. "Go upstairs and take a break. You look beat!"

I mumbled my heartfelt thanks and stumbled up the steps, not yet aware of what actually had happened to me.

I got a cup of coffee. Never before had I needed one so badly. My hands were shaking and every nerve in my body was quivering. As I drank the hot, aromatic stuff I tried to think back, to remember why I was so shaken and upset. But my last recollection before my strange, perturbed "awakening" on the job, was walking toward the divan in my apartment. The intervening period was a total blank.

Noticing a copy of the *Los Angeles Times* on one of the tables, I nervously picked it up and glanced at the date. Perspiration broke out on my forehead; the date of the paper was January 19, 1953. Seven day had elapsed of which I had absolutely no recollection! But even the date on the paper couldn't convince me. Trying to keep my voice casual, I asked a worker at a nearby table. He confirmed the date on the newspaper.

My body was bathed in cold perspiration. I was on the edge of panic as I sat there, my hands trembling so that I could hardly take a sip of coffee.

I couldn't believe that seven days and nights had passed, leaving not a trace of memory in my mind.

Later in the afternoon when I was feeling a little better I went back downstairs on the job. But it was a real effort to behave in a normal, rational manner with my thoughts in turmoil. Cautiously and discreetly I questioned Dave and other fellow workers about those seven previous days. From their replies I gathered that I had been on the job every day and had apparently behaved in my usual manner until my strange "awakening" and violent outburst that afternoon.

At home I didn't mention my inexplicable loss of memory to Mabel. And apparently she had noticed nothing unusual in my behavior during that entire week. It seemed that in every way I had behaved in my accustomed manner. I had eaten my meals, slept, gone to and from work and helped Mabel out at the Snack Bar, as usual. It was fantastically incredible!

I told no one what had happened to me. But in my own mind I was utterly baffled and deeply troubled about those seven lost days out of my life. Imagine yourself in my place. Suppose that for an entire week your waking consciousness had been obliterated so that you could not remember a single event. Wouldn't you be deeply disturbed? Wouldn't you begin to wonder if you might not be psychopathic? In all sincerity I can tell that you would, for those were my own panic-stricken thoughts.

But as the days passed I gradually settled down

into the routine of daily life. Often I tried hard to regain the memory of those seven lost days, but it seemed hopeless.

Months passed and I had about decided that for those seven days I had suffered from complete loss of memory. Except for the disquieting thoughts and vivid dreams, I had no intimation of what was coming until that memorable night in the first week in September, 1953.

I was feeling unusually restless that evening. Shortly after ten o'clock I went out for a walk. As always, my feet seemed involuntarily to carry me toward the Hyperion Avenue Freeway Bridge. In its dark, mysterious shadows I always found a kind of spiritual peace and comfort, for it was there I had met and talked with Neptune, the man from another world!

I was thinking of these things as I clambered down the concrete embankment into the almost dry bed of the Los Angeles River. Walking over to the spot where Neptune had talked with me, I sat down disconsolately upon the ground. I rested my head upon the stone where he had sat, and gazed thoughtfully up into the heavens and thought of the spiraling, endless wonders of the universe. Lost in reverie, a feeling of deep inner peace and tranquillity came over me. Noisy, clattering Earth with all of its troubles, dissensions and animosities seemed remote and relatively unimportant.

As my thoughts drifted pleasantly, I felt again the odd sensation which was always my first awareness of space visitors. But I was deeply puzzled, for Neptune had last told me: "We will return, Orfeo; but not to you."

Nevertheless the odd tingling in my arms and back of my neck was unmistakable. Hopefully, my eyes scanned the heavens. I saw nothing that in any way resembled a saucer. The intensity of the vibration increased, dimming the awareness of my conscious mind much as it had the night I had first encountered the saucer.

As in a dream my thoughts drifted back to that mysterious Monday afternoon six months before when, feeling much as I did now, I had walked toward the divan to take a nap. An astonishing thing was happening: I was beginning to remember, faintly, hazily, at first, like the sun's golden rays breaking through black clouds.

As memory flooded back I clearly recalled again that Monday afternoon. I was walking toward the divan . . . my eyes were so heavy I could scarcely keep them open. In a daze I sank down upon the divan and immediately fell into a deep sleep!

Only now I could remember waking from that sleep! My awakening was in a strange and wonderful world! I was no longer upon Earth; some fantastic transition had taken place. I awoke in a huge, fabulously beautiful room; a room the substance of which glowed ethereally with soft, exquisite colors. I was lying upon a luxurious couch, or lounge. Half awake, I glanced down at my body — but it was not

familiar! My body was never so perfectly proportioned or of so fine coloring and texture.

I noticed that I was wearing only a fine white
garment, closely fitted and covering my chest, torso
and upper part of my thighs. A finely wrought gold
belt was about my waist. Although the belt appeared
to be made of heavy links of embossed gold, it was
without weight. My new body felt amazingly light
and ethereal and vibrant with life.

Full consciousness did not come to me at once.
My first thoughts upon waking in that shining world
were nebulous. Somehow the thought persisted in
my mind that I was recovering from a long and
serious illness. Thus I reclined there in a kind of
pleasant lethargy as one does who has been very ill.
Random thoughts drifted in my consciousness.
Everything was so new and different and yet it was
hauntingly familiar. My handsome new body was
not my body, and yet it was! The exquisite room
with its ethereal, softly glowing colors was like
nothing ever dreamed of upon Earth, and yet somehow it was not strange and alien to me. Only one
thing seemed unfamiliar: far away outside the huge,
windowless room I could hear the continuous rumble of distant thunder. Oddly enough the thunder
did not fill me with apprehension as had always
been the case in the past.

Gradually the dark mists began clearing from
my mind. Incredible memories were coming back
to me; memories of another world, a different people — another life! Lost horizons, deep-buried mem-

ories, forgotten vistas were surfacing to my consciousness.

"I remember this world!" I thought rapturously. "I remember it in the same way that a condemned prisoner remembers the sunshine, the trees, the flowers of the outside world after an eternity chained in a dark and odious prison. This is my real world, my true body. I have been lost in a dimension called Time and a captive in a forbidding land called Earth. But now, somehow, I have come home. All is serenity, peace, harmony and indescribable beauty here. The only disturbing factor is a troublesome half-memory of an unhappy shadow named Orfeo, a bondsman in a prison-world of materiality called Earth.

As the disturbing thoughts of this lost Orfeo troubled me, a portion of one wall noiselessly divided making an imposing doorway, and a woman entered. She was dazzlingly beautiful. Somehow my mind understood that she was the one in whose charge I was placed, even as I also understood that the mysterious door opened and closed automatically by means of electro-magnetic controls.

She looked down at me and smiled warmly. Her beauty was breath-taking. She was dressed simply in a kind of Grecian gown of glowing silvery-white substance; her hair was golden and fell in soft waves about her shoulders; her eyes were extremely large, expressive and deep blue. Soft shimmering colors played continuously about her, apparently varying with every slight change of her thought or mood.

Hauntingly, the thought was in my mind that I remembered her from somewhere. She seemed to sense my perplexity and reassuringly said that I was looking very well and would soon be up and about. Then she touched a control on a crystal cabinet near my bed. In response a large section of the opposite wall opened revealing a huge mirror. I looked into its crystal depths, but the man I saw was not Orfeo; nor yet was he a stranger to me. Paradoxically, I remembered and yet I didn't remember!

"I have gained weight," I remarked, not knowing just why I made such a statement, then added: "Also, I feel much better now."

She smiled and replied: "On the contrary, you have lost weight. According to all Earthly standards you are now almost weightless."

Her strange words puzzled me. I glanced down at my body which appeared to be solidly substantial in addition to being much larger and more finely proportioned.

"It's all a matter of the scale of vibration in which you are functioning," she explained. "The vibratory rate of dense matter which makes up the planet Earth is extremely low, hence Earthly bodies are sluggish, dense and cumbersome. Vibratory rates here are quite high and matter so tenuous that it would seem non-existent were you in a dense physical body. Because you are now in a body of a corresponding vibratory rate, the phenomena of this world is as real to you as your Earth world."

As I listened to her speak, I thought I remembered her name. "You are Lyra?" I said half questioningly.

She nodded her head.

I was about to ask her about herself when I was conscious again of the continuous, low rumble of thunder from outside. I became curious to go out of doors and look around. Turning to Lyra, I asked: "May I go outside now?"

She shook her head. "You are not yet strong enough, but I promise that before the seventh day you shall see all, Neptune."

Her words startled me. Why had she called me Neptune? I wondered. I was not Neptune; neither was Neptune ill! And what did she mean by the seventh day?

I was about to ask her these questions when she turned and looked expectantly toward the far wall. In a moment the mysterious door appeared and a tall, strikingly handsome man entered. It was Orion! In some confused way I recognized him at once and felt a surge of affection for him in my heart. As with Lyra, shimmering waves of translucent color played about him, seemingly reflecting his thoughts. He smiled warmly and said: "We have missed you, Neptune."

I brushed my hand across my eyes in a dazed way as I replied: "But I am not Neptune; there is some mistake."

"Are you certain?" he asked gently. "You will recall that Neptune was the name you gave to our brother who first contacted you upon Earth. That name has always held a strange, deep significance for you, perhaps because it was once your own name."

As he spoke the odd realization possessed me that he was indeed speaking the truth. In their world, I was, or had once been, Neptune! "But the other Neptune?" I asked. "Who, then, is he?"

Orion glanced at Lyra and a scintillating wave of golden light enfolded them both. Orion replied slowly: "With us names are of little significance. The brother of whom you speak was in the illusion of the past known as Astra, but in the higher octaves of light, individualized aspects such as you know upon Earth are non-existent. Even now as we manifest in this most tenuous of material states of being, you are not aware of us in our true eternal aspect. We are, you might say in terms of Earth, staging a dress-show reception for you, our lost brother. Before the Destruction our existence was much as you see it now; that it why you seem to remember all of this. In that phase of the time dimension you were known as Neptune."

'Something was wrong, terribly wrong, somewhere. I thought. If only I could remember clearly . . . but everything was so confused. As I gazed at those two superbly magnificent beings standing side by side enveloped in shimmering waves of golden light, I felt intuitively that I had known them well, sometime, somewhere! I had known them on an equal level — I had been one of them! But now they were like gods to me, and I a straggler, somehow far, far behind them, my mind deluded by a loathsome illness. I pressed my hands to my eyes, trying with all of my strength to remember something important — and terrible — that I had forgotten.

Neither of them spoke. Lyra took a white wafer from the crystal cabinet while Orion poured a sparkling liquid into a lavender crystal goblet. These they handed to me. I ate the delicately flavored wafer and drank the delicious beverage. I felt renewed vitality and strength flow through my body and with it a dreamy languor of mind. Lyra and Orion smiled upon me and the scintillating waves of golden light reached out from them and enfolded me in a warm comforting glow.

"Sleep for a while, Neptune," Lyra murmured softly. Then the mysterious door appeared and they left arm in arm, leaving me alone. The light in the room dimmed and waves of soft, exquisite music flowed from the walls. I fell into a deep dreamless sleep.

When I awoke light was streaming brilliantly into the room. One entire wall had miraculously vanished revealing an outer balcony. I sat up and looked out beyond the balcony upon an incredibly wonderful and fantastic world. It was radiant with light and yet there appeared to be a heavy moving cloudbank overhead. Continuous sheet lightning flashed through the rainbow-hued clouds and the constant rumble of distant thunder was slightly louder. Also, I saw brilliant slow-moving fireballs, bollides, vari-colored flares and showers of brilliant sparks.

I was deeply puzzled, for all of this phenomena did not seem at all familiar as had so many other things in this world. I jumped up from the couch and ran out onto the broad balcony, marveling at the wonderful feeling of lightness and vibrant strength in my body.

What a glorious world I looked upon! A dream world, beyond the wildest flight of imagination. Ethereal, scintillating color everywhere. Fantastically beautiful buildings constructed of a kind of crystal-plastic substance that quivered with continuously changing color hues. As I watched, windows, doors, balconies and stairs appeared and just as miraculously disappeared in the shining facades of the buildings. The grass, trees and flowers sparkled with living colors that seemed almost to glow with a light of their own.

I caught my breath in awe. And yet, somehow, it was familiar; a world I had once known, and forgotten! A few statuesque and majestically beautiful people were walking in the pedestrian lanes. No vehicles of any type were visible. Then I saw Lyra and Orion conversing with each other near a large circular flower garden, almost directly below me. They both looked up and smiled, calling out a friendly greeting. I ran down and joined them exclaiming: "What a magnificent world!"

"Do you remember it, Neptune?" Lyra asked gently.

I hesitated, then replied: "Much is familiar, but other things are not. I can't recall the lightning and the constant thunder. And the horizon appears to be only about a mile distant and it should be — I seem to remember it was almost limitless!"

For a moment there was deep silence. Lyra glanced questioningly at Orion and a look of deep pain crossed their faces as the golden waves of irridescent light about them changed to misty purple. I realized immediately I had said the wrong thing.

Lyra touched a crystal she held in her hand and the sound of the thunder was muffled until it was barely audible. Then drifts of exquisite harmony filled the air; the same ethereal music I had heard in my trip in the saucer — only here in this incredible world each tone also manifested in the atmosphere as waves of glowing color.

I listened and watched spellbound. Lyra and Orion sat down upon the grass and motioned for me to join them. When we were seated Lyra laid her hand tenderly upon mine and Orion put an arm about my shoulders.

Then Orion spoke, saying: "Time is a dimension as your scientists now correctly surmise. But it is only a dimension when applied to the various densities of matter. In the absolute, or non-material states of consciousness, Time is non-existent. So let us say that in one of the time frames or dimensions, there was once a planet in the solar system of Earth, called Lucifer. It was of the least material density of any of the planets. Its orbit lay between the orbits of Mars and Jupiter. Among the etheric beings, or heavenly hosts, it was called the Morning Star. Among all planets it was the most radiant planet in the universe.

"The name of the prince of this shining planet was also Lucifer, a beloved Son of God." Orion paused and the sadness deepened in his eyes. Then he continued: "Earth's legends about Lucifer and his hosts are true. Pride and arrogance grew in the heart of Lucifer and in the hearts of many Luciferians. They discovered all of the secrets of matter and also the great secret of the Creative Word. Eventually they sought to turn this omnipotent force against their brothers who were less selfish. Also against the etheric beings and the Father, or Source, for it became their desire to rule the universe. You know the rest of the legend: how Lucifer and his followers were cast down from their high estate. In simpler words, the Luciferians who were embodied then in the most attenuated manifestation of matter "fell" into embodiments in one of the most dense material evolutions, which is the animalistic evolution of Earth."

I dared not look at him as his frightening words struck dark chords of memory in my heart. "Then you mean that I . . . was one of them?" Shamed tears of realization blinded my eyes.

"Yes, Neptune," he said gently, as both he and Lyra put their arms around me.

Waves of bitter shame and sorrow flooded over me as I realized the terrible truth of Orion's words.

At last I said haltingly: "But Orion, you and Lyra and these others walking here in the garden; who are they?"

"We were among those who did not join the Luciferians in their revolt against the etheric hosts," he explained gently. "Thus although the Luciferians shattered our radiant planet in the holocaust of their war, we entered the etheric, non-material worlds in the higher octaves of light as liberated Sons of God, while the Luciferian hosts fell into the dream of mind in matter upon the dark planet of sorrows."

"But this world?" I asked in bewilderment. "Isn't it the world I half remember?"

"Yes, Neptune," Lyra said compassionately. "This is a tiny part of what is left of that world. You mentioned that many things were unfamiliar, such as the thunder and lightning and the nearness of the horizon. These conditions are new to you. For we are on one of the larger planetoids of the shattered planet Lucifer. It is only a few hundred miles in diameter, hence the nearness of the horizon. The thunder, lightning and constant play of color phenomena in the atmosphere are the result of magnetic disturbances because of the vicinity of other asteroids. The clouds you see above are not clouds as you know them upon Earth, but they serve to obscure the debris of our wrecked planet. Only rarely do we leave our etheric state of being and enter our former time frame in individualized manifestations as you see us now."

I was stunned into utter silence and the deepest sorrow. I bowed my head as I thought of the magnificent world I had lost, the great heritage I had cast away to become a bondsman chained in a steel-like dungeon of dense matter with its erroneous manifestations of sin, sickness, corruption, evil, decay and repeated deaths. Sobs wracked my body as I throught of my blinded, lost fellows of Earth. At last I murmured hesitantly: "Then all of the peoples of Earth have fallen from this former high estate?"

"Orion shook his head. "No, not all, Neptune, but vast numbers of Earthlings are former Luciferians. About the others we will explain to you later. The revelation when it comes will explain many of the enigmas of your planet."

Suddenly, a terrible thought came to me, almost causing me to collapse in horror as I recoiled from it. Stark terror was in my eyes as I looked first at Lyra and then at Orion. I dared not voice what was in my mind.

Orion, discerning my thought, shook his head and his wonderful eyes radiated sympathy and understanding as he said: "No, Neptune, have no fear, you are not in reality Lucifer. In fact you are one of the Luciferians who least wanted to join the others."

Relief flooded over me leaving me weak and shaken as I heard Orion's voice continuing: "Lucifer is presently incarnated upon Earth, but we may not disclose to you his present identity. He has incarnated many times upon Earth and every name is familiar even to grade school children. But some of those names would surprise you, for they are not what you might expect."

I sighed heavily, trying to comprehend all the shattering things which had been revealed to me by Lyra and Orion. Rather incongruously I remembered the phenomena of the flying saucers upon Earth, which caused me to ask: "But if we destroyed your great planet, why are your disks visiting Earth now? Why did Astra contact me? Why don't you leave us to the fate we deserve, each one of us buried in his individual grave of living death."

Lyra's hand gripped mine and Orion's arm tightened around my shoulders. "Love is stronger than life and deeper than the boundless depths of time and space," he said softly. "While our brothers are lost in the hell of unreality and turn their blinded, imploring eyes to the mute heavens, we can never forget them. We intercede unceasingly for your peoples' liberation. Thus today every bondsman upon Earth has within himself the power through the mystery of the Etheric Christ Spirit to cancel his captivity.

"Eventually all of mankind deep-drowned in Time and Matter, will surface to reality when they recognize their basic unity of being. When man is for man honestly and sincerely and not selfishly arrayed against himself, the hour of deliverance from the underworld will be close at hand. We wait now beyond the great, sad river of Time and Sorrows with open arms and hearts to receive among us our lost and prodigal brothers in that great day when they rejoin us as liberated Sons of God.

"Our disks, or saucers as Earthmen term them, are in your space-time frame as harbingers of mankind's coming resurrection from the living death. Although our disks are essentially etheric; that is, non-material, they are controlled in such a way that they can almost instantaneously attract substance to take on any degree of material density necessary. Various other types of space craft are now permitted to visit Earth for certain purposes. These are from other worlds and also space islands of various densities of matter. Some are on the borderline between materiality and non-materiality. But all are operated by intelligences highly spiritual in nature. All are on a mission of love to their brothers of the Dark World, but mankind's understanding of their ultimate intent and purpose will only become fully apparent further along in Earth's Time Dimension. We do not say that there are no negatives in the universe who have not attained primitive modes of space travel, but at present Earth is fully protected from these by both cosmic law and the etheric hosts."

When Orion finished speaking there was silence. I sat with bowed head and contrite heart as realization of the full import of his words came to me. As Neptune, fleetingly restored to my lost immortal state, I saw that we of Earth are in reality in an underworld of illusion where we mistake false shadows for reality and dream selfish dreams of separateness from our brothers.

As these thoughts were in my mind the ringing of musical chimes sounded from the sea-green building. As though this was a signal everyone arose and entered the building. Orion led us to a large dining hall. Five men and five women were already there standing at their places at a huge table. At one end of the table was a cross wing with three vacant places. Orion indicated that I should take the middle place while he and Lyra seated themselves on either side of me.

It was an exquisite room and although there appeared to be no direct source of light the room was brilliantly lighted; the substance and colors of the room and everything in it seemed to glow with a soft, radiant light of their own. Vaguely, I seemed to remember the other persons present and they spoke to me as to an old friend. It was soon apparent, however, that the conversation was for my sole benefit as it was obvious that everyone else exchanged thoughts telepathically. As they did so irridescent clouds of color about them changed swiftly in shimmering hues and patterns.

No servants waited upon the table. Yet it was laid out exquisitely with the most delicate plates and shimmering silverware. On each plate were three portions. A triangle portion of pale amber; a square portion of varying shades of green; and a round portion of lavendar. The beverage was clear and sparkling in a crystal goblet. These strange delicacies were the most delicious and delicately flavored foods I had ever tasted. And the sparkling drink seemed to give immediate renewed strength and energy.

When the splendid meal was finished and everyone was preparing to leave the table, I turned and looked at Lyra. Suddenly, I was fully aware for the first time of all her exquisite feminine beauty and loveliness. Involuntarily, a wave of desire for her swept over me. She turned away from me and all conversation in the room ceased. I glanced hastily about; all of the others were standing silently with bowed heads. On an opposite wall I saw my reflection in a huge mirror and embarrassment flooded over me as I saw an ugly mottled red and black cloud enveloping my head and shoulders.

I felt impure and unworthy to be in that shining assemblage. The others left quietly, but I had the comforting feeling of their deep sympathy for me and their understanding for my human weakness. Also, I had the strong telepathic impression that sexual desire is merely another of the erroneous manifestations of materiality. Upon Earth it is neither wrong nor sinful in any of its manifestations except when it is used for selfish, destructive and cruel purposes. If motivated by love, altruism and unselfishness the sexual appetite is no more erroneous than any of mankind's other desires. But in the higher spiritual worlds it is non-existent.

Orion touched my arm as we were leaving the

hall. "We understand," he said kindly. "It is nothing, as you realize now."

I smiled gratefully at him. But I felt tired and very sleepy. He and Lyra accompanied me to my room where I lay down upon the couch. They sat beside me until I fell into a deep sleep.

When I awoke I was alone. I walked outside onto the terrace, but the grounds were deserted. For a long while I stood there alone on the balcony marveling at that fantastically beautiful world. Apparently it was a world of eternal youth, eternal spring and eternal day. The rainbow-hued clouds were always moving overhead shot with soft waves of sheet lightning, and the far-away echo of thunder never entirely ceased. The trees, flowers and grass were miracles of color, fire and light which in comparison made the remembered counterfeits of Earth seem like gross, dull shadows.

As I stood there marveling, I saw Lyra come out of the adjoining building. She called a warm greeting. I saw she was holding a small crystal object in her hand. When she joined me she said mysteriously: "This is the seventh Earth day and through ourselves we shall take you back."

Her strange, beautiful eyes were upon me, seeming to look through and beyond me. She did not address me either as Neptune, or Orfeo. This saddened me, for it made me realize that I was now a stranger and an imposter in their shining world.

Understanding my thought, she put her hand gently over mine and I saw a mist of tears in her eyes. Then she raised the odd crystal in her hand to her forehead. As though in magic response, a flood of beautiful melody arose from the sea-green building; not the ethereal music of their world, but a hauntingly sad and familiar strain. I recognized the sublime melody of the Bach-Gounod "Ave Maria". Tears flowed unrestrainedly down my cheeks for a half-remembered, sad people who dwelt in a strange shadowed region called Earth.

Softly she said: "You will remember this, Orfeo."

That name sounded strange upon her lips; like the name of an utter stranger. I bowed my head in bitter regret for Neptune who was, and who now was not — and for the false shadow of Orfeo who is! Confused and perturbed I turned hastily from her and hurried into my room. Somehow I had the feeling that the secret of liberation lay in the mysterious crystal panel near my couch.

But as I reached eagerly for the controls on the panel, I felt a gentle restraining hand upon my arm. I turned and looked into Lyra's wonderful eyes shining with sympathy, compassion and purest love. My own heart swiftly responded. Then suddenly, miraculously we were as one being, enfolded in an embrace of the spirit untouched by sensuality or carnality. Intuitively, I remembered that this was the embrace of spirit, shared by all of those in the light of God's infinite love throughout the entire universe. What a tragedy, I thought, that I and my lost brothers of Earth know mostly only the counterfeit embrace of sexual desire and animal passion.

At that moment Orion came in the door and as he stood transfixed, his vibrant love too enfolded us in its pure, golden unselfish light. All boundaries of self were lost in a unity of being. "Our lost brother is home at last," he said softly.

After a while Orion and Lyra seated themselves near the strange crystal control panel and I rested upon the lounge. Orion touched a crystal disk and immediately an entire wall of the room opened up into a huge three-dimensional void. The room darkened and I saw the void a magnificent view into outer space. But all of space was shining with light; the stars and suns glowed with a deep reddish glow and only the planets appeared of varying degrees of darkness. The scene was focussing upon an unfamiliar part of the heavens. A sun and a number of encircling planets came into view.

Then the scene centered upon a single planet in this unknown solar system. It was a smug, sleek planet and apparently as efficient as a billiard ball. But it was exceedingly dark in tone and surrounded with concentric waves of deep gray. A tangible vibration or emanation came from it; evil, unpleasant and utterly without inspiration or hope. Approaching this world I saw a glowing red dot with a long, misty tail. The fiery dot seemed irresistibly attracted to the dark world. The two collided in a spectacular fiery display. I felt Lyra's hand upon mine as she whispered. "It is an immutable law of the cosmos that too great a preponderance of evil inevitably results in self-destruction and a new beginning."

The scene shifted to a different part of the universe. Another dark, misty world came in view, although it was not as dark as the first world. About this world there was a vibrant feeling of life and hope. But again I saw a fatalistic fiery red dot approaching and it was evident that this world too was doomed. I shuddered to think of conditions upon that planet at that moment of doom. But then I held my breath as I beheld two tiny dots coming forth from that world apparently to intercept the fiery comet. Intuitively I realized that the dots were remotely controlled by intelligent beings upon the planet who were concentrating the magnetic impulses of the dots upon the comet. Suddenly the comet exploded leaving the world unscathed. I breathed a sigh of relief.

Once more the scene shifted and focused upon a third world. Obviously, this was an "in-between" world, neither as dark and hopeless as the first, nor yet as light and inspired as the second. To the left of this planet appeared another smaller body — I recognized it as our moon and the planet as Earth. From the planet several tiny space ships went out to the moon and did not return. Then a tiny fleet of space craft went out to the moon, but some of these returned to Earth.

Suddenly, terrifyingly, to the right of the planet Earth, appeared the red, fiery dot of cosmic doom. Rapidly it increased in size leaving behind it a fiery tail of flame. It was evident that the comet was being drawn irresistibly toward Earth. Neither Lyra nor Orion spoke, but a strange voice said: "In the Time Dimension of Earth it is now the year 1986."

I shuddered and waited anxiously, but the portentous scene slowly faded from the screen. I turned excitedly to Orion. "But what happens to Earth?"

Orion and Lyra both looked compassionately at me as Orion gently replied. "That depends entirely upon your brothers of Earth and their progress in unity, understanding and brotherly love during the time period left them between the so-called now and the year 1986. All spiritual help possible will be given them, not only by ourselves but by others from all parts of the universe. We believe that they and their world will be saved, but in no time frame, or dimension, is the future ever written irrevocably. If they bring upon themselves self-destruction of their planet through too great a preponderance of evil there, it will mean another fall for the entities of Earth into even denser meshes of materiality and unreality. As you love your brothers of Earth, Orfeo, fight to your dying breath to help them toward a world of love, light and unity."

With those awful and awesome words, he got up and slowly walked from the room, leaving me alone with Lyra.

She smiled gently into my eyes and touched the mysterious crystal panel. Immediately the incredible, huge, three-dimensional screen became active again. But no longer were we looking into the

boundless depths of space and time. Instead, I saw
the familiar outlines of the Lockheed plant in Burbank. There was the shop in which I worked. The
scene shifted inside the plant. I saw the radomes
and my working companions, Dave Donnegan and
Richard Butterfield. An unpleasant sensation came
over me as though I were fainting, as though I were
fading into the huge screen and becoming an active
part of the scene I was viewing. Terrified, I turned
to call to Lyra, but she was no longer there, only a
mist. Then I blacked out!

My next conscious perception was my strange
"awakening" on the job at Lockheed with all of my
incredible experiences of those seven days seemingly utterly obliterated from my mind.

Thus six months passed with only hazy, troublesome intimations of what had happened to me in
those seven lost days. But that night as I rested my
head upon the rock down in the Los Angeles River
bed, it all came back to me crystal clear. Also, I
remembered again my frightening, bewildered
"awakening" upon Earth in the Lockheed plant,
my terrible revulsion with everything I saw upon
Earth as compared with the wonder world I had
left, although as yet only my higher consciousness
fully understood.

I remembered my fellow workers, Dave Donnegan and Richard Butterfield and their reactions to
my strange behavior and apparently unreasoning
outburst. In the greater scope of my new understanding I realized even more clearly how nobly

they had caught me up and sustained me by their own strength through those critical moments. It was so clearly evident to me then that both Dave and Richard had the same basic inherent qualities of goodness and nobility as those godlike beings of that other world. They are both simple, humble men, average workers like myself, yet *potential gods!* If only they and others like them *knew* and could *realize* their *divinity,* their kinship with God and the greater world of *true reality!* If every man and woman upon Earth could but grasp the great essential basic truth that *we are all one and an integral part of God,* then indeed all of mankind's hard trials and bitter tribulations would be over. Yes, if only in the abstract we could momentarily attain this illumination, the heavy chains of material bondage would fall from our burdened bodies and our counterfeit world of shadows would vanish in true light.

Today, I believe with all of my heart, soul and body in my brothers of Earth. Because of the innate goodness, honesty, nobility and helpful fellowship of the countless other men and women of good will like Dave Donnegan and Richard Butterfield, my undying faith in and love for humanity is forever instilled. Even though our greater brothers of that shining, lost, wonder world should offer to take me back to my former place among them, I should have to refuse. My lot is forever with my fellows of Earth! I will fight courageously with them and for them in the undying belief that the good in our hearts will triumph over the evil. In the conviction that every human being upon Earth, trapped in eternity and granted only one small awareness of life at a time, will be liberated from our prison cells of unreality and attain again our high estate as liberated sons of God.

NOTE: The language spoken by the beings of that other world was neither my familiar English nor Italian, but another language which I fully understood and remembered while with them. But today my conscious mind recalls their language only as a meaningless jumble of strange words, although I have a full understanding in my own language of all that passed between us. I can clearly recall only a few words of that other language. Those words were spoken to me by Lyra when she first came into the room. I am certain she said, "Un doz e pez lo" (or something very similar), meaning "No, you have lost weight."

CHAPTER IX

THE TRIP EAST

Memories, fantastically beautiful memories of that other infinitely greater lost world, haunted me for days. I was like a different person. In the light of my new understanding my conception of all things was changed. I viewed everything from a new perspective. Thus I felt more than ever like a stranger here upon Earth.

One afternoon when I was in downtown Los Angeles I stood on a street corner and watched the hurrying throngs of people. All were so earnestly intent upon personal ambitions, pleasures, frivolities, worries and personal problems and so completely wrapped up in their own private worlds. Few even so much as noticed their fellow-beings on the streets. It was as though each person lived in a world apart; encased in a tomb of separateness and living death. Like shadows they hurried busily on their separate ways lost in dreams of unreality.

I realized that in truth each went his way alone; even those nearest and dearest to him never really touched the deeper core of his aloneness. This is the tragedy of mortality. Things seem pleasant enough on the surface. Earth with its flowers, trees, sunshine; the cities with their paved streets and fine buildings; the trim houses with their neat lawns — all appear fair enough. But it is like a mirage, for the material world is a prison world where each man is a bondsman locked in a prison cell. The prison cells cannot be opened from without.

Greatly saddened, I took my car from the parking lot and drove home. A storm was brewing and already a fine mist of rain was in the air. I left my car at home and walked down by the Los Angeles River where the waters were beginning to flow in the dry and dusty riverbed.

All of nature seemed waiting, quiet and tremulous, for the life-giving drops of precious water that would drench the sun-baked land and give new life to the dying trees and parched hills.

The dense clouds were dark and ominous overhead. How symbolic, I thought, of our isolation from the rest of the universe. Spiritual intelligences throughout time and space dwell in unity, communicating throughout the universe, all a part of the great harmony of the Father; but man here on his tiny planet is cut off from contact with those other worlds and fully content to vision himself grandiosely as the highest intelligence in the universe.

If only we could realize how wrong we are! We exist here on our world in a kind of solitary confinement. Our much vaunted atmosphere is one of the bars that prevents us escaping from our prison world. Also, to a great extent, it prevents contact with outside intelligences; for most of our radio and television waves are bounced back down to us by the many layers of ionized gases in our stratosphere and beyond. Hence it is much more difficult for us here on this planet to establish outer space contacts than for most other planets.

Why is this so? Why are we so completely isolated and cut off from contact with the rest of the universe?

I turned for home as the full fury of the storm broke. An onslaught of wind lashed the trees, stripping the dead leaves and branches from them. The rain came down in torrents and it was one of the rare occasions when lightning flashed in the California sky and the thunder rumbled ominously. At each flash of lightning my entire body quivered in pain. I reached home soaking wet and went to bed.

In the following weeks I continued with my weekly lectures at the Hollywood Hotel, but I was dissatisfied with my effort. I felt I was reaching comparatively few people when I should be contacting so many more.

Then in September, 1953, Paul Vest's first article about my trip in the flying saucer was published in MYSTIC magazine. Immediately letters began coming from all over the United States and even from Mexico and Canada. I was amazed at the public interest and the general acceptance of my story. It appeared that intuitively many persons had been prepared for the account.

Because of the article I was contacted by long-distance telephone by a man in the East who is a well-known evangelist. His broadcasts are heard over a large radio network each week. He told me in all good faith that in answer to his prayer for guidance after reading the article in MYSTIC, he had been shown a sign in the skies. The "sign" was the sudden appearance of a flying disk phenomenon above him while he prayed. He stated that he was so deeply impressed with what he saw that he drove immediately to the State Police barracks and notified the captain of the troop. The captain also witnessed the strange phenomenon and ordered an airplane to be sent aloft to investigate. But before the plane was off the ground the phenomenon vanished. Thus, he said, he was absolutely convinced of the authenticity of my story. He invited me to visit him in the East and make a number of appearances there.

Since I had already given up my job, we were low on funds at that time. He forwarded me one hundred dollars to cover part of our expenses on the trip East. He also enclosed a contract in which he agreed to pay me for each lecture. My purpose in going East was to reach a much greater audience, but even ,the humblest of God's creatures must have sustenance for their bodies. And surely a workman, even in God's work, is worthy of his hire.

Most of the audiences in the east were enthusiastic and highly receptive to the message of the saucers. I was happy in the belief that I had sown many seeds of understanding about the space visitors. But the minister of the gospel on whose word I had made the trip, failed me completely. He has not up until the present time (one year later) paid me for my expense and time. In fact, he was content to desert me in the East far from home and relatives and leave me stranded there penniless. His name? Does it matter?

The final lecture in Buffalo was the most successful of any of the engagements. People came from as far away as Canada, completely filling the large auditorium. Thus, from a material standpoint Christianity had thrown me from the heights, but spiritually it had sustained me stronger than ever. Also, I was beginning to learn an important lesson. The hypocrites will invariably crucify, but the truly faithful will always redeem. Actually, the hypocrites far outnumber the true. But God and only one is indeed a vast majority. Similarly, space visitors and a few are also a majority. The absolute truth of these last two statements are forever settled in my own mind.

Without funds and stranded in the East, we finally got financial help from relatives, and also an invitation to visit our folks back in New Jersey. Our spirits, which had dropped to a low ebb, began to pick up. Thus we were in almost a joyful, holiday mood as the boys, Mabel and I piled the suitcases into the car and headed for Trenton. We stayed with my father-in-law, Alfred Borgianini, on Kuser Road, close to the spot where I had once sent aloft balloons with the mold cultures in personal experiments, not knowing my work was being observed.

Our reunion with family and friends was a joyful one. We were invited everywhere and were kept out almost every night until a late hour. We quickly forgot our hardships and disappointments of the past weeks and joined in the happy, pulsating life around us. But I certainly never dreamed that there, close to my old home, I should have another experience with the extra-terrestrials.

CHAPTER X

NEPTUNE AGAIN AND PHENOMENA

IN NEW JERSEY

One evening in December about midnight I was returning to "Pop's" place alone. Pop Borgianini lives on the outskirts of town in a pleasant suburban area of average homes and small acreage farms. Clouds were overhead, but it was not a particularly dark night as there was considerable reflected light from the city.

I drove into the yard and parked my car in my usual spot. As I sat in the car for a moment breathing the clean, fresh air and looking out over the twinkling lights of the countryside, I heard a familiar voice call my name. Surprised, I glanced around to see a tall, well-built figure approaching from a shadowed corner of the yard. Because I was so completely unprepared for such a meeting, it took me a moment to collect my thoughts and realize that the familiar voice could be none other than that of Neptune. As he came nearer to the car I could see him fairly well in the soft light. He appeared just as he had that night down by the Los Angeles River. His closely-fitted "uniform" wavered like restless clouds of light and shadow.

But somehow I felt altogether different meeting him now; there was none of the eerie feeling I had experienced upon the occasion of our first meeting.

He seemed to feel much as I did, for he said cheer-fully: "A merry Christmas to you, Orfeo." His warm, radiant smile was still the same, as was his noble bearing and everything else about him; yet I was able to comprehend and understand him so much more easily now. I wondered, had he descend-ed closer to my level, or had I, since my strange "awakening" in that other world, risen nearer to his?

He answered the question for me. "You are in-deed a dweller in two worlds now, Orfeo. Some-times it is difficult for you to determine which world is substance and which is shadow, or if both are not merely differing degrees of substance. But you have done well, considering all that you have been through in these last two years. In reality you are now liberated from your planet, Earth and are a citizen of the cosmos. For seven Earth days you were conscious in our world as it existed in Time, while I kept watch over your physical body as it performed it normal duties here on Earth. Thus in a way I am a part of you even as you are a part of me. There now exist eternal bonds of understanding between us."

As he spoke, I thought of a puzzling statement he had made to me during our first meeting. It was that memorable night down by the Los Angeles River. I distinctly remembered that he'd said: "We shall return, dear friend, but not to you." I re-membered the words so well because I had been so saddened to hear them. Thus as I looked at him now I was thinking that his very presence there seemed to belie those words.

He smiled again and said gently: "In reality we have not returned to you, Orfeo. You came to us. When you awakened as one of us, you had come home. Don't you understand? We are not returning to the shadow, Orfeo; our lost brother has returned to us. And from our first contact with you we never in reality ever left you."

I grasped the meaning of his words, for I well knew I was no longer the same person who, confused and bewildered, had stepped half-fearfully into the saucer that night under the Hyperion Avenue Bridge. "Yes," I replied thoughtfully. "What you say is true. Earth to me now often seems like a strange land where I have been a prisoner who has forgotten his native home."

"But you are no longer a prisoner, Orfeo. You have broken the chains of matter. Thus can you realize that you were a prisoner — and that realization is all important. The vast majority of Earth's people never dream of their true status."

He paused, and after a moment I said: "You know, of course, about the lecture tour . . ."

"We were with you through it all," he replied. "Several times you had a definite awareness of our presence. But even so, it was all a bitter disappointment to you. On more than one occasion you thought it was the end of all your hopes and plans. But there is no end to anything, Orfeo . . . ever!

Nor should you let the material aspects of any situation perturb you, such as the Reverend "X's" failure in your hour of need. Upon Earth there are wheels within wheels. When one wheel fails, another is forced to bear a heavier load. But the wheel that fails will be required to carry a double load further along in Time. That is a law of Earth. Thus accept all with courage and equanimity."

After a moment, while I pondered his words, he continued: "On the West Coast all is comparatively quiet now. But the road is opening. Many have attained tenuous, new understandings. The governments of the world could say much more to the people about the saucer situation, but they will not until the zero hour is at hand. Are not those your thoughts?"

I did not reply, but smiled at him, for I knew that for a period of time I could have revealed many things about the saucer situation that were believed to be well hidden — and thus have stolen the thunder from many. Instead it was given to them as their very own even as the rains and the sunshine, but they failed the trust.

He continued slowly and thoughtfully: "The days that are to come upon Earth are known to me, but they are as yet mercifully veiled from you and from your fellows. This I can tell you: the hour of tragedy is close on Earth. In history it will be known as 'The Great Accident'. Wide devastation, suffering and the death of many will result from it. Per-

. haps you can guess how Man himself will be the direct cause of 'The Great Accident'.

"It is permitted only as a last hope of waking mankind to the terrible realization of the ghastly price he will pay if he enters the bloody holocaust of Armageddon. There is still a slight chance to avert the War of Desolation for in the Time dimension nothing is absolute. But if the horror of the War of the End of an Age shall come, our multitudes are at hand to aid all of those not spiritually arrayed against us."

I bowed my head and as afar off I heard echoes of the hauntingly beautiful music of that Lost World; sad music as though thousands of angelic voices were joined in a hymn of sorrow.

At last Neptune said softly: "My brother of the universe, be not dismayed. Remember it is always darkest before the dawn. And the dawn is close for Earth. So close that the first glorious rays are already breaking for many in your world. Already we can behold the shining reality of your great world of tomorrow — a world of brotherly love and fellowship when Man is for Man and bound in unity through the love of the Father. The clouds on the horizon will pass quickly and tomorrow the sorrows seem only as dreams of darkness. We of the universe wait for the dawning of Earth's great tomorrow when we can welcome the children of Earth into our midst. Let our love and our faith sustain you and your fellows. And now, goodnight, Orfeo."

With those words, a silvery mist obscured the outlines of his figure. He faded away into almost complete transparency, although I could hear the echo of his footsteps as he walked away. It was obvious that his figure could definitely gain in density at will and also gather and resolve light.

As in a daze I got slowly out of the car and went inside the house surprised to hear so much noise and commotion in the dining room and kitchen. When I entered I saw that the room was full of people. Many of our relatives were there as well as some of the neighbors. Everyone seemed to be excited and was talking and gesticulating. No sooner was I inside than Mabel and several of the others rushed up and started telling me what they had seen off to the northeast a few miles away.

From the explanations I gathered that they had seen what appeared to be two round, large lights apparently playing tag with each other below the cloud bank. The phenomenon had continued for about fifteen minutes. They were still so excited that they interrupted each other to describe the capering antics of the two strange lights.

But having just come inside from my profound experience with Neptune, I was not in the least excited by their reports. They could not understand why I was so calm and disinterested. It irritated them slightly. My sister-in-law, Alice, asked, a little peevishly, if I didn't believe what they told me. All of them were obviously let down because the news appeared to have no effect upon me.

Of course I believed every word they said. Why

shouldn't I? One of my brothers-in-law had nearly broken a leg jumping out of a high kitchen window to get a better look at the strange lights. I believed them all right, but I could not permit them to project their interpretations and reactions upon me. When they finally quieted down some I said: "Look how excited and close to hysteria you all are tonight. Suppose the Air Force should release the full impact of certain saucer news straight from the shoulder? Millions of people everywhere would begin reacting just as you are, only to a greater degree. Yet none of you are quite certain of what you saw. If the Air Force released certain definite information, there would be no uncertainty. It could be the beginning of national panic that no amount of sane reasoning could quell. Thus the public gets news releases of flying saucer activity, but immediately a retraction or an explanation in terms of known phenomena follows. A dampener of some sort is always placed upon such news. Never in the history of our country has any office, individual or branch of the government handled news items in such a manner. The whole picture actually, is clearly before our eyes. And yet where does it get us? Still no flying saucers landing cozily in our back yards. Small wonder the present policy is not to publicize saucer stories."

Finally, almost at dawn, the excitement quieted down sufficiently for us to get to bed and get a few hours sleep. The following day the newspapers carried reports of the sighting of strange "lights" by many people throughout the countryside. No one had "hallucinations". No one saw just the usual type of lights. After all, masses of people don't to-day excitedly report street lamps, searchlight beams, etc. How stupid can we get?

But the news was far too sensational! It had to have a damper put upon it quickly in one way or another. Fortunately for the flying saucer experts, it was about time for Earth to pass through a meteor stream.

Three days later, an old friend of mine, the local weatherman, made an official pronunciamento, blithely explaining away the lights in a simple and perfectly reasonable manner. They were, of course, meteors, he announced in the papers. We were expecting a shower of meteors, weren't we? Well, what else could those lights be but meteors? Official sources never fail!

Good, old Mr. White, the weatherman, God bless him. I like him. I have always liked him. Even though he always lost in his guesses with me, with the local farmers, and with most other prognosticators concerning the condition of the weather on the following day. I have seen him lose for weeks in succession and never guess the weather correctly in one instance. This delightful game has been going on for years. The weather perversely remains pretty unpredictable even for the experts.

But coming out so badly in his rounds with the weather, the weatherman had no compunctions in tackling the flying saucers.

Thus Mr. White, or his press secretary, is still attempting to explain away those confounded "meteors" to a number of stubborn individuals. For it just so happened there was an overcast of clouds and mist that night. Two of the mysterious lights played around with each other below the clouds for nearly fifteen minutes. They were round, large, white lights without the fiery tails respectable meteors are supposed to flaunt. Now, Mr. White, these people, dozen of them, are either falsefiers, or else they saw something out of this world which cannot be neatly explained away by your pat little explanation.

What quality within you caused you to offer the explanation in the first place? Did you see and study the phenomenon as did those others? Could it possibly be that you were prompted by disturbing feelings of uncertainty, insecurity and fear of the unknown? You just wanted someone to say those lights weren't there, so badly that you finally up and said it yourself!

But enough for our good friend, the weatherman. Like the weather, he's always with us.

Elsewhere the overall saucer picture was improving. It appeared the road was being opened from new angles. By the end of December, 1953 hundreds of new reports of saucer activity were coming in. Also there was the significant news of Canada's construction of a flying saucer observatory. It was located near Ottawa and known as Project Magnet. Essentially a UFO detection station, it was being equipped with complex and expensive electronic equipment which were designed to detect gamma rays, magnetic fluctuations and gravity or mass changes in the atmosphere. Thus the instruments could detect immediately any magnetically controlled disks in the vicinity. The engineer in charge of the project, Wilbert B. Smith, stated that he believes there is a 95% probability that the UFOs do exist. He based his report upon the massive files of data on well-authenticated sightings on hand.

Also, Canada was actually building a jet-propelled flying saucer. Another step in the right direction. There were many new developments in the United States, but most of it was hush-hush stuff. But the flood of reports from all over the world could not be ignored. Great Britain officially recognized the phenomena. Other countries heard from were Australia, New Zealand, Sweden, Norway, France, Germany, Brazil, Japan, Denmark and many more.

But of course there were still the "die-hards", those who flatly refused to recognize the realities of this century. Of this last subversive element I met a number on my tour of the East. Failing in their desperate attempts to convert me to Communism and slant my talks along the Party Line, they invariably defiantly demanded: "Well then, just what do you think is wrong with Communism?"

My reply was invariably the same: "Absolutely everything is wrong with it! There is not one iota of right in it. Its only possible good is its ability to awaken to action the positive forces of good which are often sleeping. Communism is the negation of all that is honest and good in the world and in humanity. They would enslave the human mind. Their obstructiveness is willful and planned. We must eventually meet this murderous element at Armageddon; when it will be victory for one side or the other. Good will triumph, or evil! Every entity in this world and the adjoining planes is now aligned definitely upon one side or the other. No matter what the outcome of the conflict, the positive element of good will ultimately attain a greater life and progression; whereas the negative will meet death, destruction and a new beginning in a more hostile environment. As you have made your choice, so be it!

Shortly before the New Year we left New Jersey and set out on the long journey home to Los Angeles. We drove leisurely and enjoyed the scenery, so different from our perpetual springtime of Southern California. The boys especially got a kick out of it. Between Carlsbad Caverns and El Paso our car stalled on the desert. It was late at night and we were many miles from a town. I remember Mabel remarking dejectedly as she shivered in the cold night air: "Well, Orfie, we could certainly use some help from those flying saucers right now."

I smiled at her attempt at humor in our unfortunate situation. But the boys hopefully scanned the heavens as though aid might be imminent. As for myself, I had learned that the space visitors never in any way interfere in mundane affairs.

Thus, of course, no glowing disk obligingly appeared to succor us. A very much down-to-earth truck
did, however, and we eventually made it to the next
town where I discovered that a tiny wire had become disconnected and short circuited the electrical
system.

I felt rather foolish as I thought of how grandiosely
I had been expounding the principle of infinite
electro-magnetic power in flying saucers, but was
utterly helpless in handling a simple problem in the
electrical generation of my own car. The experience caused me to remind myself sharply that I
could actually get lost between worlds, unless I kept
my feet firmly upon terra firma, my home as of now.

Back home in Los Angeles I had the unpleasant
feeling of being definitely let down. And I didn't
know where to begin to start picking up the threads
of my previous activities. The entire situation appeared as being rather futile and much too big for
me, to have any effect. But several days after our
return I received a phone call from Mrs. Dorothy
Russell of Manhattan Beach asking if I would give
a talk before the prominent Neptunian Club in her
city. She didn't know it, but she was responsible for
picking me up out of the depths and launching me
once more upon my mission. "Neptunian Club,"
I thought as I hung up the receiver. "Could the
name be just a coincidence?"

At Manhattan Beach I spoke before a packed club-
house. The meeting was a tremendous success and
everyone in the audience was receptive and en-

thusiastic. Additional lectures in other Western cities followed. Also, I resumed my regular weekly meetings at the Hollywood Hotel. All in all I felt things were progressing as well as I could hope. At times Mabel still urged me to "forget it all", and go back to work at Lockheed again. But I knew I couldn't ever do that. Come what may, I would tell all who would listen about the space visitors.

CHAPTER XI

I HAVE A VISION

Hundreds of volumes could never put into words all that has transpired in my life and states of consciousness within the last two years. The enthrallment, the divine ecstacy and the joyous rhapsody of breaking the chains of matter and mortal mind cannot be even dimly imagined. Yet in our sad world of pain and woe one must pay with anguish in equal degree for each upward step. Hence, I tell you in all truth that the vast majority would cringe from facing the bitter sufferings and trials that have been my lot in this and previous lives before I attained the revelation of the infinite majesty of reality.

Today I can see in the higher octaves of light and hence understand the unreality of all my sufferings. All that I endured was the illusion of pain super-induced by the limited vision of my material mind in those periods when the supposed suffering occurred. It is perfectly clear to me now that physical pain, mental anguish, material obstructions, defeats, disease, adversaries and adversities exist only within limited material consciousness. My sufferings *seem* to be real in the erroneous three-dimensional physical plane of existence and within the time dimension. But in the light of the truth of my eternal self, the supposed suffering is in reality non-existent.

To many people what I have just said may sound like an absurd paradox, but thousands of others will understand my meaning, for they themselves have been through this evolutionary process in varying degrees. As one emerges into the truth of spirit from false material consciousness an entire new concept of materiality is attained. Increasing numbers of persons will go through some stages of this understanding within the next few years, for material adversity in all of its many aspects will be stepped up to a considerable degree. We are at the beginning of the Days of Sorrow!

Today it rained again in Los Angeles. Water is flowing in the bed of the Los Angeles River. In the late afternoon the sky began clearing. As evening was coming on I walked down to the river, stood on the bridge and looked over the concrete guard rail.

I looked down upon the spot where I had sat at Neptune's feet. A great wave of emotion swept over me shaking me to the innermost depths of my being. "Ah, Neptune," I thought, "do you, too, feel the poignant tragedy of Earth when you set foot upon this ground?"

As in a dream then I heard a gentle voice saying: "Consider Earth's solar system and the many other solar systems throughout the universe. Are not the planetary units of these solar systems the true archetypes of the flying disks? The disks, like the planets, are round, suspended in ether, propelled by ether waves and magnetic light from system to system.

"Many of the entities of the various worlds throughout the cosmos have discovered the basic principles of the universe and hence have been enabled to travel in the various solar systems. Their actions and thoughts are in perfect harmony and full accord with the laws of the cosmos. They respect the rights of all worlds and of all individuals everywhere. But most of all do they respect and act in perfect harmony with the infinite mind in which they live and move and have their being.

"Speak to all you see, Orfeo. Tell them of the undiscovered wonders of the material universe and of the infinitely greater wonders beyond. You will speak with the truth of harmonious love, which is the only real authority. In reality, all is light; eternal light throughout space, the reverse of the testimony of the material mind. Within the spiritual universe only the points behind the planets give the illusion of darkness where a mere trifle of light is occulted by the body of the planet. But in reality darkness is only an illusion created by the false thoughts of material consciousness. All who come out of the illusion of darkness into the light will never again be lost in the illusion. Throughout the universe entities wait eagerly to aid your brothers of Earth, but the choice is up to each individual, for every mortal being has been equally endowed with free will. You, Orfeo, have walked through the valley of the shadow of death and emerged into eternal light. Help others to do likewise."

For a while then there was silence as inexpressible

thoughts and emotions flooded my consciousness. At last the voice continued: "Behold, two thousand years are rolled back tonight before your eyes."

As I listened to the incredibly beautiful voice, my eyes were upon a revolving aircraft beacon light on a nearby hill. While I watched, the red and green of the beacon light resolved into a soft amber color and the amber flame in turn became a shining sword. Slowly the sword was transfigured into a cross and upon it I saw the figure of a Man in death.

While I watched spellbound, He awakened and looked down from the cross upon me. His face broke into a radiant smile, and with no effort at all He stepped down from the cross and walked toward me in shining beauty. I looked again at the cross and it was only a shadow that splintered into nothingness.

As He walked toward me I heard a tremendous chorus of voices singing joyous music, and floods of happiness overflowed my heart.

I looked again and He was standing just beyond the wall of the bridge. I beheld Him more clearly than the light of day, yet in no detail, as when one looks upon the sun and beholds only radiance.

I heard His voice inquiring gently: "What is your name?"

I replied: "Matthew." But even as I spoke I corrected myself mentally. Matthew was my middle name.

He said: "You chose that name yourself when you

were a small child. You wanted no other name but that one. Do you remember?"

I nodded my head, for I did indeed remember.

And then I heard him say: "But Matthew was a publican. And were you not as a publican before May 23, 1952?"

I bowed my head in shame before Him, for I realized that I was indeed as a publican and perhaps even worse.

In a voice filled with infinite tenderness then, He said: "Do not be ashamed, Orfeo. Don't you remember I always chose the publicans and harlots over self-righteous hypocrites?"

Veils were dropping from my eyes and I was remembering details of a life lived many lives ago back in Time. I hid my face from His sight and tears of shame and remorse blinded my sight.

"Do not weep, Orfeo," He said gently. "That is all in the past now. But I am with you today even as I was with you then. Tell mankind that I live and love them today even as I did two thousand years ago when I walked the shores of Galilea. But tell men that to know me today when soon I shall again appear publicly upon Earth they must find me *first* within their own hearts."

He paused and my eyes could no longer bear to look upon the radiance of His beauty. And then he said: "Remember, Orfeo, wherein it was revealed to you not long ago that beings from other worlds now walk upon the Earth. Each is a double of the other and they have of their own free will entered the valley of sorrows that is Earth, to help mankind. One moderates another when too little is accomplished or when certain limits are exceeded. No man upon Earth shall know them except the ones to whom they reveal themselves. And who publicly claims to be one, is not at all. Only by their fruits may they be known. This is the beginning of the mysteries of the New Age."

Slowly then, the shining vision before me faded until He was no longer there. Only a soft shining green light remained pervading the atmosphere. I stood for a long while in silence as the heart of creation enfolded me in infinite peace.

At last, I was just turning to go home when I heard a familiar voice call to me: "Orfeo, what are you thinking?"

I turned and saw Neptune standing on the banks of the river, close to the spot where we had sat some eighteen months before.

As I tried to collect my thoughts, I replied: "Don't you know what I'm thinking, Neptune? Or am I lost to you now?"

"No, Orfeo, you shall never be lost to me," he answered. "But there are sublime moments when no one may penetrate another's world of thought. Or perhaps I should say that those who would do so are not able, and those who could would under no circumstances do so."

"I understand, Neptune," I said. "The ultimates are for all, but in moments of realization one becomes a universe within himself and hence is protected by the powers of the cosmos. You then are as we and we are as you, children together in the Father's infinite worlds of manifestation." When I had finished speaking, I was surprised at my own words. It did not seem possible that I could be saying such things to Neptune. And yet I had said them and he was smiling at me as though my thoughts were his very own.

But as I looked at him he vanished from my sight. And suddenly I felt alone and very small and insignificant. I ran along the bridge to the pathway leading down to the spot where Neptune had been standing. He was nowhere to be seen; but in the archway of the bridge I saw again the softly glowing outlines of a flying disk.

The door of the saucer was open and while I was wondering whether or not to enter, a woman appeared in the entrance. It was Lyra, more exquisitely beautiful than I had remembered her. Smiling at me she stepped from the craft and it seemed that the blades of grass trembled mysteriously and the wind stirred, vibrant with strange music that was barely audible. All of nature seemed to stir as though touched by a caressing hand. She walked slowly toward me and her shining white gown fairly scintillated as though in protest to the dense, irrational atmosphere of Earth. All of the infinite love for man in his Christly potential which I was feeling at that moment, was blissfully culminated in the wonder of her presence. She who encompassed all love, all compassion and all understanding and whose radiant eyes were a benediction.

When she was closer to me I saw that her gown shimmered like restlessly drifting moonbeams, just as had Neptune's darker uniform here in our dense atmosphere. In her hand she was holding a glass which she held out to me saying: "Drink from this glass, Orfeo, and your normal consciousness shall return. You will then be an equal with your own fellows and able to show them the way."

Uncertainly, I took the crystal goblet from her, but I dreaded to drink from it, for I feared that she and Neptune and all the world might recede forever from me.

She smiled again and a soft golden light enfolded her just as in her world. "Everything we have done with you both in your world and in ours has been adequately moderated. Hence all that you experienced in the higher worlds has been compensated to a similar degree in the lower. Thus be neither glad nor sorry for all that has thus far been granted to you. Remember, love is understanding and understanding is love throughout the universe. Hence love is the constant of all worlds. By love I mean only selfless love and not the carnality which is often mistaken here on Earth for love. Love is infinite freedom. Drink from this glass and know peace again within yourself."

Slowly I raised the glass to my lips and drank. When I had finished, I let the glass fall to the ground, but heard no sound of it. The drink seemed to clear my head and to give me a feeling of strength and normalcy. Lyra had not faded as I feared she might. Rather she appeared to be more real than ever before.

"We must go now, Orfeo," she said gently.

Her words greatly saddened me for I dreaded to think of her leaving me. But only for a moment, for I immediately realized none of them would ever in reality leave me again. Slowly, I said: "I understand what you meant about the drink, Lyra. For now I feel that I am at home again upon Earth as I used to be. I shall never forget you, Lyra, for I am a part of you and Neptune and Orion and your world, even as you are a part of me. I know now there is no death other than that which men upon Earth call life. Also, I know there is no evil act in the world which cannot be atoned. Lyra, you shall be with me always."

With those words I bowed my head and when I looked again she was gone as though she had simply faded into nothingness. Only an exquisite fragrance was left permeating the air as if bowers of invisible flowers were everywhere.

When I thought to look for the outline of the saucer under the arch of the bridge, it was no longer there. I stood for a time in the soft reflected light of the evening, at peace with myself and all things. Although they were gone, I no longer felt alone, for in reality I knew I could never be alone again in this life or any life to come.

I turned and walked home. When I opened the

front door I felt a tremendous wave of warmth and peace that awaited me in my own house. The boys were busy with some magazines and Mabel was sitting in a rocker sewing buttons on one of my shirts. When I came in she looked up and smiled and for the first time in months I seemed to see her clearly for the wonderful person she is. With the light from a floor lamp falling on her hair and in her simple dress she looked like a Botticelli madonna. Within her I beheld all the mystery and wonder of womanhood: she was like a reflection of Lyra, the highest potential of feminine evolution.

"We've missed you, Orfie," Mabel said. "Where have you been?"

"Oh, just down by the river, Mae," I replied as I kissed her more tenderly than I had in months.

She rewarded me with a smile as she said: "It's so good to have you home again."

Her words increasing my feeling of peace and serenity, for I was home again. Lyra and Neptune had indeed given me back to my family.

I walked over and turned on the radio for news. Busy, eager voices were enthusiastically staccatoing the latest horrors of the terrible devastation of the recent H-Bomb test. News of the tremendous discovery of a hideous nerve gas, a pint of which would kill an entire city of people. Earthquakes. The rumble of war in Indo-China and other danger spots. Unrest. Anxiety. Murders. Suicides. Fear. More reports of the subtle evil forces insidiously at work here among us weaving their own devious webs of deception and obstruction. Man against man to the bitter end! Oh God, how long, I thought. How long before the compassionate Earth shudders in revulsion — shaking the stars!

As I switched off the radio I realized more than ever how much work there is to be done. In reality this age of discord and stark materialism is already in the past and we have entered into the New Age. Many spiritually awakened persons today are well aware of the true state of affairs. To all of these men and women of honest heart and sincerity of purpose and to all of those in past ages who have worked against fearful and bitter odds for the good of man and the betterment of his lot upon Earth I have dedicated my life.

Now is the hour! The great promise of the golden dawn is breaking. The light of its revelations is imminent in religion, medicine, scientific research and all other fields of human endeavor. Fulfillment of the great promise of the ages is at hand. Space visitors are the harbingers of dawn upon Earth.

Mistakes shall occur, but we shall correct them. When war, tribulation and cataclysm come, even these shall quickly pass. For the rainbow of eternal promise is now in the heavens. The shining hosts of the great brotherhood of the spiritual federation of the universe are waiting to receive us into their midst and to let us know them as they really are. The highest flights of our imagination and our wildest dreams cannot compare with the wonderful world of reality that lies ahead in Time for us.

The universe is you — and you are the universe. The infinite numbers of entities in God's mansions in the cosmos are essentially as you and I as we are and have ever been in true spiritual reality. If we will but waken from our dark dreams of death they will lavish life and beauty upon us. Thus choose for yourself. There is no in-between road today. We have come to the dividing of the way and it is now one path or the other for every entity upon Earth and its adjoining planes of manifestation.

CHAPTER XII

HOW TO KNOW A FLYING SAUCER

A flying saucer can manifest its presence in many ways. A few persons whose neurological sensitivity is similar to mine may detect a saucer's presence by physical symptoms such as I have described earlier in this book.

Only recently Mr. Vernon Tyler, Director of the Santa Monica Municipal Airport, had such an experience. He relates that on Wednesday evening March 24, 1954, he retired early. About ten o'clock he was almost asleep when he felt an odd prickling sensation along the back of his neck and down his arms and spine. He said the hair on the back of his neck felt as though it were standing up which reminded him of some sort of electrical phenomenon. He was wide awake immediately and filled with a peculiar sense of urgency as though he were in contact with something or someone. He jumped out of bed and went to the window and looked outside, but saw nothing.

He walked around the room restlessly for some time with the distinct feeling that someone wanted to contact him. At last he went to bed again and finally fell asleep. The next morning a friend, Fred Carlyle, phoned him and wanted to know what was going on over Tyler's house about ten o'clock the night before. Startled, Tyler questioned him. Carlyle said that he and his family had watched four strange objects, or lights, directly over Tyler's house maneuvering in an incredible manner and without sound for some time.

That same day similar reports were given to the *Santa Monica Outlook* newspaper by Mrs. Genevieve Downer and her husband, Steven; Lillian Colbary and her daughter, Marilyn, and Mr. and Mrs. Arthur Swalge, all of whom saw the mysterious objects over Tyler's house. It later developed that many other persons in the neighborhood had witnessed the phenomenon, although they hadn't phoned the newspaper.

But of all the persons in that residential area, Tyler was the only one known to have experienced the unusual physical symptoms. Later on, when he read the article I had written about my physical symptoms in saucer contacts, he stated that his sensations were identical.

Thus physical reaction to the electro-magnetic qualities of a saucer are unusual. If you experience them, you may be certain your body is attuned to extra-sensory perceptions.

Since a crystal disk may be as small as two inches in diameter and can penetrate material densities, a disk may be present in a hall or room at any time and may or may not be visible to the eye. In the darkness they sometimes appear as softly glowing floating lights which appear and vanish suddenly.

Many persons have seen a flying saucer and have failed to recognize it as such. Hence we are going to

list here the most common manifestations in order
that you may better judge a UFO should you see
one:

THE ROVING STAR: One of the most common
appearances of the disks and the least reported are
those which merely rove around in the night sky.
Often they are mistaken for airplane lights or a
star. But if you hear no sound of an airplane motor
and the "star" appears to move, then you well may
be observing a disk.

THE METEOR: If you see a "meteor" that leaves
no fiery trail behind it, or one that changes color
peculiarly, watch it closely. Also any "meteor" that
appears to "hover", or one that changes its course
suddenly to an upward sweep, or to an angled turn,
is probably a saucer. Also any large round fireball
that follows a definite horizontal path and then
bursts in a brilliant shower of sparks, either with or
without noise, is definitely a particular type of saucer phenomenon. Similar to the latter is a huge
"meteor" that appears to explode in a blinding flash
lighting up an entire area, but without sound. These
are all manifestations of UFOs.

THE SILVERY DISK: This one cannot be mistaken. At first glance it appears as an airplane, but
something causes you to give it a second glance.
Then you see it can't possibly be an airplane for it
is round and spherelike. Or it may appear oval-
shaped or in the form of a half sphere. It may appear to pulsate or if you cannot actually see the
pulsation you have the definite impression that it is

pulsating, for the effect is registered more upon your nerves than upon your retina.

Often there appears to be a darker center to this silvery, metallic-appearing disk. Also, the disk may seem to wobble through the air or weave along like a seasick man. The darker center may appear to move off-center. Sometimes it continues to move all over the surface of the disk as though in rhythm with the odd wobbling motion of the disk.

What is this dark area in the silvery disk? It is the control beam focus, the beam connecting the disk to the one in control. This extra-terrestrial type of "radar" beam has the disk so strongly gripped that the very motion of the disk is vectored by the beam. The same mechanism holds for the incredible right angle turns. It is like a yo-yo which is held firmly by the string.

WHEEL WITHIN WHEEL: This type also has been frequently sighted. The strange effect of rotation of wheels-within-wheels is manifested for different purposes. As in the case of many other types of manifestation, it has been used by extra-terrestrials to impress a certain individual or group of individuals. If you see a saucer of any type, you may rest assured you have been "chosen" for the sighting for some specific reason.

The multi-rotation effect in this type of UFO is caused by actual disk-within-disk rotation. The peculiar visual effects result from the conversion of magnetic force into energy focused in the disk.

The energy must be converted and dissipated, so

it is discharged at the outer edges of the saucer.
When those in control wish to make a display for
the benefit of an individual or group of persons,
they merely "gun-it-up" and the static electric discharge then shows as flames, darting streaks, fireballs, or similar phenomena. They can also direct
this force behind the object, giving the impression
that the disk is jet-propelled.

Magnetic propulsion was scoffed at just a year ago
and some still scoff even though model disks in our
laboratories have been made to respond to this force
to a limited degree. In reality, this field has become
one of the most vital and secret research projects in
the United States, Canada and certain other nations,
one of which has advanced further than we like to
think.

Incidentally, the magnetic principle explains any
behavior of flying saucers ever reported. Proceed-
ing from the magnetic principle of propulsion and
its dynamics, we would ultimately discover the
secrets of constructing a flying saucer of a primitive
type. This very fact has proven the existence of the
saucers beyond any and all doubt.

Yet insofar as the extra-terrestrials are concerned,
final proof of the saucers had to come to us from the
actual testimony of sightings and experiences. This
was finally accomplished. Work was immediately
commenced in laboratories of various governmental
agencies on the magnetic principles of propulsion.
And then what happened? All official mention of
saucers vanished on all fronts. Insofar as the public

is concerned, the saucers just aren't any more, although hundreds of reports continue to come in. Only Frank Edwards, the ex-A. F. of L. newscaster from Washington, D. C. and a few other courageous souls mention the true facts.

All official statements are now made along academic and conservative lines mentioning our own researches and "discoveries" in the fields of projected missiles, magnetic researches etc.

What a strange paradox indeed. The very ones who fought valiantly for recognition of the saucers are literally given the final *coup-de-grace;* whereas those who fought it tooth and nail are busily engaged upon electro-magnetic researches.

The space visitors have revealed much, enough to give us ideas to go ahead scientifically in new and heretofore unknown directions and potentials, but unless we learn the ethics that go hand-in-hand with mechanics, all of our knowledge will be taken from us. The space visitors are trying to teach us as we would teach little children, but smart little boys that we are we just won't learn.

THE TRIANGULAR FLAME: Many have seen this type of UFO manifestation. The triangular flame is no more than a total configuration of a number of disks in formation. These are made to discharge electric energy in that shape, and the disks become invisible while the entire configuration shows up. Or, it can also be a semi-material object with the powerplant of the disk incorporated within it. Any of these are very simple to produce for those in the remote control station which, of course, is the mother ship. Within laboratories here on Earth some of this phenomena can now be produced in limited degrees. But no one is talking and certainly not behind the iron curtain.

DISAPPEARING AIRPLANE: This type is a projection both visual and auditory, but the mechanics are too complex to go into here. All we can say is that if an airplane attracts your attention irresistibly and seems to hold you by a strange, intangible force, it may be a disk-projection. You may be absolutely certain of this if it has a dull, flat surface that does not reflect sunlight and, of course, when you see it suddenly vanish before your eyes.

THE TORPEDO: The torpedo, or cigar shaped craft is rare. You probably would be first attracted by its seemingly swift, silent flight. It is shaped something like a dirigible but is much more graceful in appearance. Portholes may be visible in this type, or they may not, depending upon whether they were opened at the time of the sighting. It may hover motionless in the air, or suddenly disappear into nothingness. But of this much you can be certain if ever you are lucky enough to see such a craft: you were meant to see it for a definite reason that will either be clear to you at the time, or later on. These are the master ships of space and are often hundreds of feet in length, although some of the smaller ones may be no larger than a large airplane's hull.

THE FLYING SAUCER: This object is spherical,

hemispherical, or just disk shaped. It is the motive shape and is a utility craft of many uses. Its size can vary from less than two inches to miles in diameter. The larger ones out in space usually have plastic canopies and serve sometimes as passenger ships.

Thus we have listed all of the types of extra-terrestrial craft which have thus far manifested in our atmosphere. Any of them may be flatly opaque, or may instantaneously be rendered so transparent that the best mortal vision cannot see them. In reality, they are most active when they are invisible. It is thus that they photograph and record words, thoughts and deeds, check births and deaths and re-incarnating egos, record undercurrent trends in governments, etc. They are the silent observers and recorders of all.

Although one may contact you in absolute silence and be invisible to your physical sight, some moment in the future you may have a "spiritual awakening", when you will remember the saucer's vigil. The awakening may be years after the actual contact was in effect. It seems the extra-terrestrials really "favor" such persons by keeping them entirely undisturbed by visual experiences. Today these millions of persons are those who *know* space visitors are here. They do not know how they know it, but they accept it anyway. Most have never seen a saucer knowingly or have caught only an uncertain glimpse of one. But for them the day is coming when through extra-dimensional perception, they will "remember" and their eyes will be opened. Several of the finest contacts to date are of this nature.

On the other extreme are those who have seen spectacular displays of UFOs and go their way skeptical and unimpressed. These are the persons the space visitors can never touch. They live in a dark world of their own.

Because of the seemingly harsh planetary laws prevailing upon Earth, any type of spiritual growth involves pain. Thus both God and nature appear to hurt most those they love. So it is and must inevitably be with space visitors. The ascent from Hell is not easy! So as God tries with suffering those who are dearest to Him, so must the extra-terrestrials to a degree. In the over-all picture no one is ignored except those who wish to be ignored. The choice is up to the individual.

CHAPTER XIII

STRUCTURE AND MOTIVE FORCES

OF FLYING DISKS

Contrary to present concepts, we do not conquer space, we cooperate with it. A good dancer does not force steps and movements into a rhythm. He feels the music and cooperates with it. A good pilot does not rip through the air. He cooperates with its dynamic forces. Birds accomplish this naturally.

Notice fish in a bowl or tank of water. They glide and dive in streamlined beauty as they feel every slightest movement and vibration of the water. Their motions are in perfect harmony with their environment. Throughout all of nature there is no conquest of the elements. There is only harmony and cooperation with the laws of the elements. The creature who defies these laws must inevitably suffer.

Space is today the most challenging frontier. It is also one of the most dangerous. Any wrong interpretation or calculation of space will result in immediate and violent reaction.

Space ships do not carry walls of lead many feet thick. The cosmic rays in outer space could easily penetrate these. In reality space ship hulls are not much more than many layers of skins something like plywood but made of plastic-crystal substance. Some layers are positive ionized, and some negative. These are insulated from each other with neutral layers between them.

The approaching cosmic rays are rendered unstable by the field of magnetism constantly maintained around the ship. Upon reaching the hull of the ship they are completely shattered. Then the positive and negative charges are absorbed by the many-phased charges of the various skins of the hull. Thus, not one cosmic ray should penetrate inside. This is harmonic cooperation with nature's forces.

Harmony and cooperation are positive in effect. Man's first space ships may evolve from his present limited knowledge and still navigate space to some extent, following many of nature's laws. But many of those first experimental craft will meet with destruction and failure because only the highest degree of harmony and the finest perception can survive space navigation.

First, it is well to understand that atoms are not in reality whirling particles of energy. They are simply "bubbles" in the ether. Also, light rays are merely portions of these bubbles, but in elongations; thus in reality appearing as darting fissures, or splits in the ether.

There are endless variations of magnetic fields, or fluxes in the entire universe. From the bubbles (atoms) they bounce away in all directions, producing magnetic spheres. From the light rays they proceed away at right angles to the rays so that magnetic vortices accompany the rays. Cosmic rays produce their own magnetic wakes in their paths. Thus the ether is in constant motion at all times in all places.

The flying saucers utilize all these forms of energy. They direct in precise control the conversions of the energies, and use the same forces as means of attraction and/or repulsion in the endless sea of the ether. Thus, their directors can use magnetic and gravitational forces far beyond our wildest imagination.

They do not require our Earth's fields. Indeed, Earth's field and ether slip-stream are in their way. In outer space the flying disks flow and seem to dance in gracious beauty.

Many of the flying saucers that we have seen in our skies are actually crystal disks, grown in chemical baths. Like the stem and capillaries of a leaf or flower, all the functioning systems are grown into it. Therefore these systems could be utterly invisible. These systems would include the conducting wires spiralled from the center to the extreme outer edge, the spirals becoming narrower in cone shape. At the extreme edge they come to less than pinpoint, and the excess electrons are forced into "ground" from these points. This function can be stepped up until the very disk seems to give off flames. Usually, however, we see it only as a fuzzy halo fringe around the object.

The crystal property of the flying disks refines all the electro-magnetic and corpuscular energies into varying frequencies and wave lengths. Among the etheric beings, however, it is possible to create a saucer of any degree of materiality merely from a projected thought form which attracts material substance to it.

Since, however, the majority of saucers thus far sighted have been of the crystal disk type, we shall confine explanations to these alone. (Although the thought-form projections behave in a very similar manner).

CHANGING OF COLORS IN DISKS

As the crystal is stepped up by electro-magnetic energy its lattice structure undergoes definite changes which cause the disk to emit light of various colors. That we might observe this phenomenon is one of their reasons for revealing it in the skies.

The lattice of the crystal can be arrested at any attitude. When it is suspended in an attitude of transmitting, all light will pass through, and the disk becomes completely invisible.

When electric force is discharged under normal conditions, a flame, or darting lightning is visible all around the disk. Thus we see flames of all colors; also darts and streaks of fire, and in some cases, even an exhaust trail when the entire effect is directed backward or forward of the flying object.

By directing a sudden impulse of energy and resistance to the energy simultaneously into the disk, it can be made to explode into a shower of spark fragments.

RIGHT ANGLE TURNS

A flying disk is not just guided. It is completely

controlled. The master beam from the mother ship holds like a vise. This is always the case when they perform right angle and sudden turns. Thus they can assume incredible speed, and suddenly veer sharply without any damage to the disk. Every atom and molecule is vectored in the same direction at the same time. Any gravitational effects from inertia are neutralized, or non-existent.

During my trip into space in one of these crystal crafts, you will recall that I picked up a strange coin-shaped piece of metal from the floor. This piece of metal appeared to be quivering and livid in the palm of my hand: and as I held it the metal became almost glowing, as a piece of live coal, and yet it was the same temperature as my hand. Within forty minutes the metallic disk had disappeared. Apparently its elements were sublimated by some type of evaporation process. Thus, it is apparent they can explode them at any rate of speed they wish; and in a limited frequency of energy they would explode with not the least sound. Such remote control by complete vector is an accomplished fact with our space neighbors.

It should be clear now to see that they can appear to the human eye and yet never register on camera film. Or, on the other hand, they can be made to show up on film when they were not visible to the human eye.

Presented with the true, simple explanation of the flying saucers, some people find it harder than ever to accept. They prefer to cling to the ideas of impossible tons of lead shielding and all the other ponderous aspects of space ships as conform to our limited sciences, most of which will have to be discarded before we even put a ship into outer space.

FLYING DISKS — EXTRA DIMENSIONAL CAMERAS

A flying disk is maneuvering over a city, or some area of the Earth. Every living thing and all their vibrations, seen and unseen by the naked eye, are picked up by the transmitting disk, which in turn relays these impressions back to the mother ship. There it is all permanently recorded on crystal instruments in detail.

Most of these scanning and recording operations are conducted when the disks are entirely invisible to us. When we do see them, they are usually just capering for us, or for some particular individual, to whom the display reveals a message, or an awakening. Both, spiritual and physical evolution upon Earth is timed, and is in gradual steps. Space visitors are in no hurry, and they enter in the evolution gradually, in the timing permitted them by cosmic rhythm and law.

Yes, indeed, the flying disks are both receiving and sending units. They are three-dimensional camera, television, radio, and motive entities, all in one. In fact, they are practically a synthetic brain, lacking only consciousness itself. Their manipulation is intrinsic and seemingly boundless. We on Earth are close to arriving at this technology in the realm of hypothesis, at least.

CHAPTER XIV

THE TRUE NATURE OF THE

SAUCER MYSTERY

Only a short time ago we should have been obliged to go to great lengths to convince most people of the actual existence of flying saucers. Today, fortunately, we are spared the indignity of such futile efforts. The saucers definitely are here, and the majority of persons now are willing to admit this awesome fact. But the interpretation of flying saucer phenomena is an entirely different matter. As strange as it seems, the mystery of the unidentified flying objects is little nearer a solution than it was in 1947 when several flyers first made reports of sighting nine of the disks near Seattle.

Since then impressive files of new data have been amassed, but much of this evidence is so contradictory and bewildering that instead of offering a solution to the problem, the new facts have only rendered it more complex. Significantly enough, the most erroneous conceptions have been ponderously expounded by those whose every thought and utterance is in slavish conformity with the known laws of physics and the analytical laboratory method of approach. Insofar as the saucers are concerned, the "I know it all because I can prove it" attitude, whether uttered or insinuated, has only indicated with absolute certainty that no infinitesimal part of the true answer is known.

Today it is almost impossible to ignore the saucers, and those who attempt to do so are motivated in no small degree by egoistic personal prejudices. Yet to accept them unreservedly as coming from outer space is still considered by many to be somehow laughable. Thus have the saucers become a ready target for jokes and laughter. It is well that this is so, for a measure of humor is always a safety factor in any human struggle to new heights of understanding. The coming of the saucers will ultimately prove one of the most tremendous struggles of the ages in the evolving consciousness of mankind.

The story of generic man and his history upon Earth presents a ponderously slow, painful and often bloody pageant of evolution out of evils inherent in himself. No animal is as cruel as man. The pages of history are stained with records of deeds motivated by violent intolerances, vicious hatreds, arrogant lustings for power and wealth, sadistic cruelties, connivings, treacheries and mass slaughtering of fellowmen. Thus have we evolved to our present questionable status.

Yet as in the days of the building of the ancient tower of Babel many of us arrogantly feel that we have attained dizzy pinnacles of wisdom and scientific "know-how". Whereas, from a cosmic viewpoint, we are but an innately selfish, warlike species of earthbound grubs who have only within the last few years become conscious of the boundless universe. Only during the last fifty years have we learned to build ponderous vehicles that will fly and explore a tiny way above the surface of our planet. And our first thoughts are of conquest: conquest of new planets, conquest of the moon for a space station to police the world. Even as our agile minds are busy with these thoughts, we continue to plot mutual slaughter of our own kind.

Even the dulled wings of our imaginations will not permit us to imagine that intelligent beings who inhabit other planets in the universe may not have evolved as we did through cruel animalistic natural laws of survival of the fittest, the cruelest and the most insidiously clever. Thus with the first reports of the saucers people everywhere considered with alarm a possible intrusion of space craft from other worlds. We, by our own standards, expected them to have predatory ideas of conquest and enslavement of mankind. As a result the flood of horror films of monstrous extra-terrestrial invaders has not yet ceased.

As a matter of fact, the coming of the saucers is not an intrusion of a new order on our Earth; neither was it omitted from the original plan of nature on this planet. The saucer phenomena we have thus far witnessed is an integral part of a vastly greater plan for us than our finite minds can begin to comprehend. Thus, the saucers definitely are not to be feared!

But it would be a terrifying thought to think that

we are drifting aimlessly all alone in boundless time and space upon an insignificant speck of matter we call Earth. In reality, we are not alone either during our sojourn upon this planet or in the universe. Our conscious minds, however, are so limited that we base practically all of our conclusions upon a strictly material foundation. Hence most of our conclusions are erroneous. But the secret of life we have been unable to fathom from any material viewpoint. In the final analysis even science must revert to the abstract idea of a vastly greater intelligence as the source of life. But having admitted so much, can we believe that this intelligence has long ago abandoned us here upon our ball of clay? To many it has seemed so, but only because the erroneous nature of our conscious minds is incapable of realizing mankind's true condition and state of being.

It is the will of the Creator that we perfect both our planetary home and the microcosm of our individual selves. As long as man progresses in the right direction, no matter how slowly or precariously, he shall continue to receive greater spiritual insight and a gradual broadening of material horizons in the fields of science. But each revelation of the hitherto unknown comes to us bounded by its own mystic shroud. Slowly these mystic shrouds of matter are expanding as concerns the macrocosm and ever closing in upon the atom. But as advanced as we like to think we are, in our present state of consciousness, a revelation of the true beauty be-

hind all things would shatter our conscious minds.
The eternal enigma "inside" even a humble bac-
terium enthralls the researcher and holds him spellbound. Yet, even he cannot behold its true reality!

Thus it is my sincere hope that the factual story
I have told you about my contacts with extra-terrestrial visitors will prove not only a discovery of
the true nature of the beings from out of space and
time, but perhaps the infinitely greater discovery
of your own true self and from whence you came,
why you are here, and whither you are bound.

Although my story is given in good faith, some
are bound to doubt me. For man does not trust man
because the evil inherent in the human heart so
often betrays him. Yet to many my words will
bring greater understanding and release from the
bonds of a prison. My experiences are interwoven
with the truth of man's being as inextricably as
strands of thread are a part of the fabric.

If this very day my story could be proved to every
skeptical person, the mystery of our space visitors
would be ended. And we should be ready and eager
to greet them as brothers in the infinite federation
of the universe. But ideas preponderantly spiritual
cannot now and have never been capable of proof
by material methods. Hence no material proof of
the reality of my experiences may be given to satisfy
skeptics.

First, to remove all possible fear from the idea of
space invaders, I wish to state that in the vast
majority of cases those who have conquered the

problems of space travel have progressed to, or have always existed in, a state of spiritual consciousness which we today can conceive only in the abstract. For one of the immutable laws of the cosmos is that evil projected to its limits is self-destroyed; hence too great a preponderance of evil invariably results in self-destruction and a new beginning in greater densities of matter. Evolving toward good or evil, life and brotherhood, all go forth in majesty akin to the glory of the gods of the ancients. The evolved spiritual intelligences of the planets communicate only with the graduates of other planets; none others are or may be aware of their true natures.

Today the evolution of Earth both material and spiritual has reached its most critical point. Thus chronologically speaking the hour has struck upon our planet which has not only permitted, but demanded the influx of outer space entities and their material manifestation in our sphere of consciousness. They have come as harbingers of light to do everything possible to turn the tide of destruction which threatens to engulf Earth and terminate in a new fall for man into greater darkness and bondage in heavier chains of matter.

In the space being's contacts with me there has actually been some factual evidence — almost enough to serve as proof, even to materialists. But not quite enough! The evidence has been minus that same enigmatical fraction of verification necessary in nearly every instance of saucer manifestation throughout the world — whether in case of personal experiences or with official branches of certain governments (except in a few specific cases involving spacecraft of a most primitive type from which factual and technical data have been obtained, as intended by them). And herein we find pinpointed a significant clue to the true nature and mission of space visitors. They have ingeniously enshrouded their presence in mystery; certainly not because they have any desire to be mysterious, but only because we are not sufficiently mature to bear the impact of the full revelation of even the least of our extraterrestrial visitors. Understanding of them will come eventually, but only through our own interpretations. Thus will we begin to understand in terms of our own finite and immature intelligence some of the mysteries of beings who live in worlds less erroneous than our three-dimensional, pain-pleasure, suffering-and-death sphere.

In any research, in any revelation, in any miracle when so many individuals and groups of individuals have witnessed a certain phenomenon, or some phase of that phenomenon, it is usually sufficient proof to accept as true the existence of that phenomenon. When this point is reached the boundaries of understanding usually advance further. Insofar as the saucers are concerned, we have now reached that point. Hence, I am now telling my story more completely. Parts of my story have previously appeared in the single issue of my own newspaper, *The Twentieth Century Times,* and parts have been published in MYSTIC magazine, but never before has the entire account appeared in print. Only now has the mystery of the saucer phenomena come to an apparent dead-end which requires elucidation before anything further may be gained from extra-terrestrials. In other words, this book is Earth's answer to their signals to us. I hope it will produce results.

CPSIA information can be obtained
at www.ICGtesting.com
Printed in the USA
LVHW061555240521
688335LV00002B/48